Published in 1988
by The Hamlyn Publishing Group Limited
Michelin House, 81 Fulham Road, London SW3 6RB
by arrangement with Western Publishing Company Inc,
Racine, Wisconsin, USA

ISBN 0 600 55850 9
Printed in Czechoslovakia
52 178

The material in this book has previously appeared in
Richard Scarry's Storybook Dictionary and *Best Word Book Ever*.

RICHARD SCARRY'S
Best Read and Learn Book Ever

 clock

 bell

blackboard

calendar

teacher

inkwell

map

map stand

waste-paper basket

HAMLYN

leapfrog

marbles

crawl under

sheriff

clarinet

CONTENTS

pull

kettle drums

bouncing ball

hoop rolling

drink

cornet

stand

dental nurse

eat

hacksaw

push

A B C D E
F G H I J K
L M N O P
Q R S T U
V W X Y Z

PASTE

Aa *Aa*

amazing!

aachoo

Ali Cat says "**aachoo**" when he sneezes.

able

Wiggles is **able** to reach the biscuit jar.
He can reach it. Poor Squeaky can't.

about

Pickles and the piglets are **about** to have supper.
The piglets are running **about**.
Sit at your places, piglets!

above

A mosquito is flying
above Flossie's head.
It is over her head.
Look out, Flossie!

accident

APPLES

Dingo had an **accident**. My goodness!

across

Hooligan walked **across** Smiley
to the other side of the stream.

act   acts, acted, acting

When we move or do something, we **act**.
Chips is in the **act** of sawing wood.
We also **act** when we pretend to be something.
Sneakers is **acting** as if he were a real pirate.

9

add   adds, added, adding

If you **add** one squealing piglet
and two squealing piglets,
you have three squealing piglets.

afraid

The piglets are **afraid** of the water.
Silly piglets! Soap and water won't hurt you.

after

Huckle ran **after** Squeaky.
After he caught Squeaky, he was very tired.

again

Bumbles was not able to cross
the brook the first time he tried.
He will try **again** and **again** till he crosses it.

against

Two bad cats were fighting
against each other. One pushed
the other **against** Ma Pig's clothesline.

age

Tom's **age** is five years.
He is five years old.
He received a nice present
on his birthday.

ago

Mr. Fixit dropped a hammer on his toe
a minute **ago.** He is howling now.

agree   agrees, agreed, agreeing

Maud thinks she is prettier than Molly.
Molly doesn't **agree** with her.
She doesn't think it is true.

aim aims, aimed, aiming

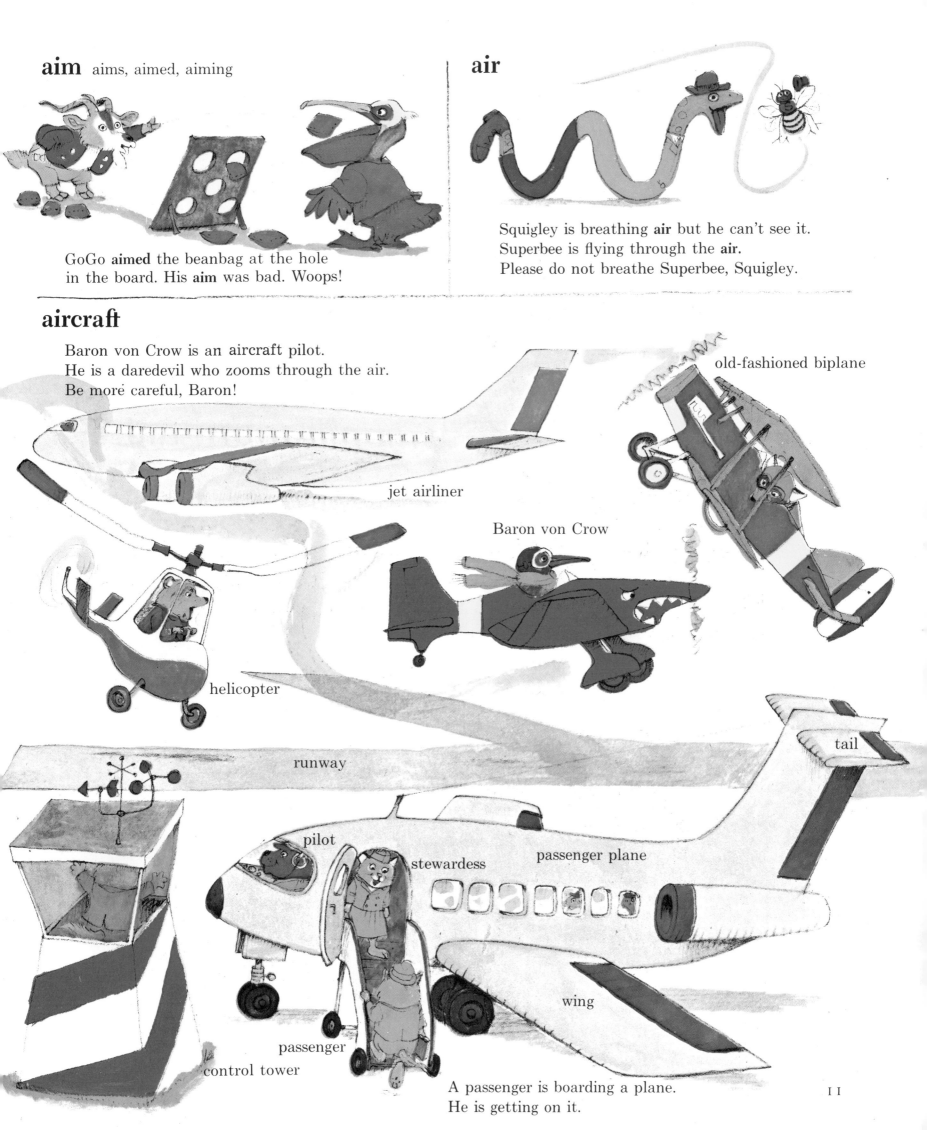

GoGo **aimed** the beanbag at the hole
in the board. His **aim** was bad. Woops!

air

Squigley is breathing **air** but he can't see it.
Superbee is flying through the **air**.
Please do not breathe Superbee, Squigley.

aircraft

Baron von Crow is an aircraft pilot.
He is a daredevil who zooms through the air.
Be more careful, Baron!

jet airliner

old-fashioned biplane

Baron von Crow

helicopter

tail

runway

pilot

stewardess

passenger plane

wing

passenger

control tower

A passenger is boarding a plane.
He is getting on it.

11

alike

The piglets are all **alike.**
They all look the same.

alive

HeeHaw has two flowers in his flower pot.
One is **alive.** It is living.
The other one is dead.

all

The beggars ate **all** of Mamma's blackberry pie.
They didn't leave any. **All** of them are happy.

almost

Father **almost** missed catching his bus.
He nearly missed it.

alone

Babykins is playing by himself. He is **alone.**
He knows mud pies aren't made with earth **alone.**
You need water, too.

along

Ali Cat walked all the way **along** the fence.
Squeaky went **along.** He went with Ali Cat.

already

Pickles has **already** finished his meal.
Already he is looking forward to his next meal.
Pickles, you can't be hungry again so soon!

also

Tom likes to make music with his bugle.
He **also** plays with his drum and cymbals.

always

Bumbles **always** wears a red cap.
He wears it at all times.

amaze amazes, amazed, amazing

Babykins **amazed** everyone when
he played the piano. He surprised them.
They didn't think he could do it.

among

Mamma divided the cake **among** the beggars.
She gave some to each of them.
Poor beggars!

angry

Bully Bobcat knocked Squeaky down.
Squeaky is very **angry.**

animal

All **animals** move about.

bee

bird

Some **animals** fly.

mouse

monkey

cat

tiger

kangaroo

pig

Some **animals** have tails.

otter

mouse

grasshopper   Some **animals** hop, jump, and run.

Some **animals** wiggle and crawl.

worm

animal

Some **animals** have horns.

bighorn sheep

chamois

gnu

reindeer

yak

antelope

kudu

musk ox

another

Badger put on a pair of trousers.
It was cold out so he put on
another pair over them.

answer answers, answered, answering

Mummy Bunny asked Flossie a question,
and Flossie told her the **answer.**
Just then the telephone rang.
Please **answer** it, Wiggles.

any

At the toy shop, Grandma told Kitty Cat
she could have **any** doll she wanted.
Tom Cat doesn't like dolls.
He likes **any** toy that makes a big noise.

anything

It is time to give Babykins his bath.
Mother is wearing her raincoat.
Babykins isn't wearing **anything**.

around

Hooligan ran **around** the pole.
He ran **around** and **around**.
He got dizzy from running in circles.

as

Pickles eats his meals
as a nice pig should.
He chews slowly **as** he eats.
As soon **as** he is finished,
he will wash the dishes,
as he will need to have them
clean for his next meal.

ask asks, asked, asking

The beggars **asked** Mamma Bear
for something to eat.
She **asked** them to wash
their faces before eating.

asleep

Babykins is **asleep**.
He is such
a nice little baby
when he is not awake.

astronaut

Baron von Crow wants to be an **astronaut**.
He wants to go to outer space.
Baron, an **astronaut** needs a spaceship, not a plane.

attention

Henny is teaching her chicks
to scratch for food. One chick is not
paying **attention.** Better listen to what mother says.

awake awakes, awoke, awaking

Babykins was asleep.
Now he is **awake.**

away

Baron von Crow flew **away**
in his aircraft. Bye bye, Baron!

Bb *Bb*

bravo!

back backs, backed, backing

Mr. Fixit parked his lorry
and went into the shop.
Now he is coming **back** to his lorry.
He has a stove on his **back.**
Oh dear! Dingo backed into
Mr. Fixit's lorry!
He smashed the **back** of it.
Now where will Mr. Fixit put the stove?

bad worse, worst

Ooch Worm likes **bad** apples.
The **worse** they are, the better he likes them.
This is the **worst** apple he's ever eaten. Yum yum!
Is Babykins being a good boy or a **bad** boy?

bag

Henny carries her hand**bag** on her arm.
She carries groceries in a paper **bag.**

baggage

When Pappa Bear goes on a trip,
he takes several suitcases.
That's a lot of **baggage.**

bake bakes, baked, baking

Mamma Bear **baked** a cake in the oven.
She forgot to take it out on time.

bandage

Hannibal hurt
his trunk.
Squeaky put
a **bandage** on it.

bank

Ma Pig keeps her money
in a big **bank**.

Pickles keeps his pennies
in a piggy **bank**.

Pa Pig was sitting
on the **bank** of the river.
Suddenly, he caught
a big fish!

barrel

Who has fallen into the pickle **barrel**?

basket

The piglets are playing
in the laundry **basket**.
What will Ma Pig say when she finds a **basket**
full of piglets?

bathroom

shower
medicine cabinet
towel
tap
soapsuds
bathtub
washbowl
bath mat
soap
comb
toothpaste
toothbrush
toilet

Big Hilda is taking a bath in the **bathroom**.

beach

Huckle is making a sand castle at the **beach**.
Don't make it too close to the water, Huckle.

bedroom

lamp

bed

pillow

blanket

sheet

Mose is sleeping in the **bedroom**.
You forgot to turn off the light, Mose.

beat

beats, beaten, beating
beater

Mother is **beating** an egg with the egg **beater**.
Babykins is **beating** a pot with a spoon.

beautiful

Captain Fishhead gave Mrs. Fishhead
a **beautiful** new hat.
It flies **beautifully** when the wind blows.

because

Brambles could not comb his hair
because a bird had built a nest in it.

before

Father Cat ate his breakfast
before he went to work in the city.

He was late for his train.
He had never been late **before**.

begin

begins, began, begun, beginning

HeeHaw is **beginning** to plant his garden.
He is just starting to put carrot seeds
in the ground. He should have **begun** sooner.

behave behaves, behaved, behaving

Some children **behave** well. Some **behave** badly.
Do you always **behave** as you should?
Do you always do the right thing? Always??

behind

Ali Cat is hiding **behind** the fence.
Squeaky is standing in front of it.

believe believes, believed, believing

The beggars said that they had not
had a bath for fifty months.
Mamma **believes** they are telling the truth.

bell

Tom is ringing a **bell** very loudly.
The next door neighbour is ringing
the door**bell** to tell him to stop.

belong belongs, belonged, belonging

The muddy footprints **belong** to Wiggles.
They are his very own.
Always try to remember that mud **belongs**
outside the house. That's where mud should be.

below

Gus is **below** Annie Ant.
He is singing
beneath her window.
O sole mio!

bend bends, bent, bending

Bumbles fell down and **bent** his skis.
Macintosh is **bending** over him
to see if he is all right.

beside

Hooligan is sitting **beside** Big Hilda.
He is sitting next to her.
Look out! Big Hilda is falling asleep.

between

An ice-cream soda is on the table **between** Maud and Molly.
They are sharing it **between** them.

big   bigger, biggest

Bully is **big**.
Squeaky is small. He wishes he were **bigger** because Bully is the **biggest** pest he knows.

bird

Birds have feathers and wings.
Look at the **birdie, birds.** Don't fly away before your picture is taken.

heron

stork

flamingo

eagle

birdie

kiwi

parrot

duck

penguin

toucan

goose

puffin

turkey

birthday

Squeaky went to Kitty's **birthday** party and fell into the ice cream.
Get out before someone eats you, Squeaky.

bite   bites, bit, bitten, biting

Pickles **bit** into the pie.
Do not take such big **bites**, Pickles!

20

blade

Annie is taking a **blade** of grass home for supper. *Bon appetit!* Good eating, Annie!

block blocks, blocked, blocking

Babykins filled the front doorway with **blocks.** He **blocked** it and Father couldn't get in.

blow blows, blew, blown, blowing

The wind **blew** Heather down the street.
The policeman **blew** his whistle.
STOP! STOP! You are speeding!
You are going too fast!

board

Chips is sawing a **board.**
Turkle and Crabbie are playing a game on a game **board.**

boat

Mr. Fixit's **boat** has a hole in the bottom.
Water is coming in through the hole and filling the **boat.** It will sink.
Mr. Fixit is drilling another hole because he thinks the water will empty out through it. Isn't he silly?

freighter

sightseeing boat

submarine

ocean liner

barge

speedboat

ferry boat

leaky rowboat

oar

yacht

body

Everyone has a **body**.
Why, even Dingo has a **body**!
Every **body** has many different parts to it.
Ali Cat and Squeaky have drawn
pictures which show the different parts.
Some of us have tails.
What kind of tail do you have?

THE HEAD

hair
ear
eye
cheek
nose
tongue
face
lips
tooth
chin

THE BODY

head
wrist
neck
shoulder
elbow
chest
arm
stomach
paw or
hand
waist
knee
claw or finger
foot
tail
leg
heel
ankle
claw or toe

mouth
teeth

TAILS

22

bone

Dingo went into a restaurant.
The waiter served him a **bone** for lunch.

book

Chief Five Cents is reading a **book**
to his little girl, Penny.

both

Flossie washed **both** her ears.
Wiggles washed only one of his.
Go and wash the other one, Wiggles!

bottom

Squeaky is at the **bottom** of the ladder.
Ali Cat is at the top. In a second
Ali is going to be at the **bottom**
of the barrel.

box

Pickles and Squeaky are eating breakfast.
Come, come, Pickles! Out of the cereal **box**!
That is no way to eat breakfast.

brave

Brambles is very **brave**.
He is not afraid to have his hair cut by the barber.
He knows that he will be even handsomer
when the barber has finished.

break breaks, broke, broken, breaking

"Don't play with my watch or you'll **break**
it," Father warns Babykins. Too late!
The watch is already **broken**.
Babykins can **break** anything.

breathe breathes, breathed, breathing

Big Hilda is **breathing** air.
Breathe in, **breathe** out.
Leave some air for Squeaky, Hilda!

bridge

Dingo drove off the **bridge** into the river.
Oh dear, Dingo! Learn to steer better.

bright brighter, brightest

How **bright** the sunlight is today!
It is much **brighter** than yesterday.
Big Hilda has the **brightest** swim suit at the beach.

bring brings, brought, bringing

Ma Pig **brings** the piglets
to the barber shop every month.

brush brushes, brushed, brushing

Brambles is **brushing** his hair with a **brush**.
He is a handsome fellow, isn't he?

bubble

Bilgy is blowing **bubbles**.
A **bubble** burst on Huckle's nose.

build builds, built, building

Chips is **building** a house.
That is *some* house, Chips!

24

building

Ali Cat is drawing pictures
of different kinds of **buildings.**
Squeaky is colouring the pictures.
Can you draw a picture of the
building you live in?

windmill

church

palace

cottage

half-timbered house

skyscraper

castle

barn

terrace houses

chalet

brick house

factory

tower

lighthouse

Squeaky
loves
Big Hilda

25

bulb

The lamp wouldn't light
so Pappa Bear put a new **bulb** in it.
He threw the old **bulb** away.

bump bumps, bumped, bumping

Dingo drove down the **bumpy** road.
He **bumped** into Mr. Fixit.

They both got **bumps** on their heads.

burn burns, burned or burnt, burning

Daddy Bunny was **burning** leaves.
Daddy **burned** his rake.
If you are not careful with fire,
you can get a bad **burn.**

busy

Haggis is **busy** cleaning out his cupboard.

but

Six sausages are on the plate
but they will not stay there for long.
Pickles will eat everything **but** the plate.

buy buys, bought, buying

Brambles is **buying** a comb at the shop.
He gives the shopkeeper money for it.

by

The beggars are going on a trip **by** train.
They have seats **by** the door.
Now they are passing **by** a toffee factory.

Cc *Cc*

clever!

---

call calls, called, calling

A young lady came to **call**.
She is **called** Big Hilda.
When Big Hilda got stuck in the chair,
Mummy **called** for help.
Soon Big Hilda was unstuck.

can could

Mose **can** stand on his head.
He is able to do it.
He **could** stay that way all day
if he wanted to. But he doesn't.

---

can

Ali Cat keeps his paint in **cans**.

---

card

Squigley and Fingers are playing a **card** game.

---

care cares, cared, caring

Kitty is taking **care**
of Babykins.
She **cares** very much
for her baby brother.
She loves him a lot.

---

carry carries, carried, carrying

Mamma Bear is going to bake bread.
She is **carrying** a bag of flour
from the larder. **Carry** it carefully, Mamma.

27

catch catches, caught, catching

Wiggles was trying to **catch** the ball.
His trousers **caught** on a twig and ripped.
Hurry home before you **catch** cold, Wiggles!

centre

Baron von Crow's plane landed
in the **centre** of the pond—right smack
in the middle of it.

change changes, changed, changing

The weather **changed** from sunny to rainy.
HeeHaw had to **change** into dry clothes.

chase chases, chased, chasing

Bully is **chasing** Squeaky.
Will Bully catch him?

chief

Chief Five Cents lives in a smoky tepee.

choose chooses, chose, chosen, choosing

Mose is **choosing** a hat to wear to the circus.
Which will he pick? Which one would you **choose**?

circle circles, circled, circling

Baron von Crow flew around in **circles**.
He ran out of petrol and stopped **circling**.

class

Ali Cat has a painting **class**.
He gives lessons in painting.

clean cleans, cleaned, cleaning
cleaner, cleanest

Sneakers is a bit **cleaner** than Wiggles.

Wiggles just **cleaned** his face and hands.

Now he must **clean** the bathroom.

clear

The glass jar is as **clear** as air.
Poor Superbee didn't even see it.

clear clears, cleared, clearing

Mamma Bear wanted to **clear** up after dinner.
But in **clearing** the table, she picked up
the tablecloth instead of a napkin.
That's one way to **clear** it quickly, Mamma.

climb climbs, climbed, climbing
climber

Babykins likes to **climb**.
He is a good **climber**.

clock

The alarm **clock** rang and
awakened Father early in the morning.
Brrrrrriinnnngggg!

close

It is **close** to bedtime.
It is nearly time for bed.
Kitty holds her doll
close to her.

close closes, closed, closing

Bilgy **closed** the door.
He slammed it shut.
Close it gently next time, Bilgy.

29

clothes

Wiggles' **clothes** are scattered all about.
Wiggles is looking for his other mitten.
It's right where you put it, Wiggles.
Why can't you hang up your **clothes** neatly
the way your sister does?

pyjamas

slippers

mittens

vest

bathing suit

cap

sweater

shirt

underwear

overalls

tie

socks

hat

plimsolls

gloves

jacket

muffler

overcoat

rain hat

boots

raincoat

galoshes

shoes

swim trunks

belt

handkerchief

stocking cap

stockings   blouse   skirt

pinafore

slip

nightgown

panties

30

cold

It is **cold** inside the refrigerator.
Pickles opened it so often he caught a **cold.**

colour colours, coloured, colouring

Ali Cat is **colouring** a picture
with his crayons. There are many
different **colours.**

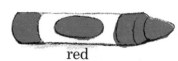
red

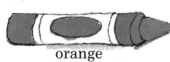
orange

yellow

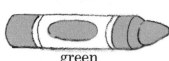
green

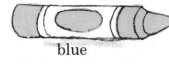
blue

purple

brown

grey

pink

black

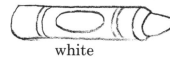
white

come comes, came, coming

Bilgy invited Pelican to **come**
to his house for a fish supper.
Pelican **came** and brought Squeaky with him.

cook cooks, cooked, cooking

Ma Pig is a good **cook.**
She is **cooking** some soup
Now how did that shoe ever get in her soup?

cool cools, cooled, cooling

Bramble's soup was too hot to eat.
He turned on the fan to **cool** it.

copy copies, copied, copying

Ali Cat wrote a word.
Squeaky **copied** it.
He wrote it just the same as Ali.

corner

Pappa Bear is waiting for a bus on the street **corner**.
There is a shoe in one **corner** of his bag.

cost costs, costing

Babykins broke his playpen.
Mother Cat asked Mr. Fixit how much money
it would **cost** to fix it.

cough coughs, coughed, coughing

Big Hilda has a bad **cough**.
Doctor Pill gave her a spoonful
of **cough** medicine to help her to stop **coughing**.

count counts, counted, counting

A number of ants have come
to Hooligan's and Hepzibah's picnic.
How many ants can you **count**?

country

HeeHaw wears farm clothes
when he is working in the **country**.
He wears his best suit when he visits the city.

cover covers, covered, covering

The **cover** will not stay
on Ma's cooking pot.
She is **covering** her eyes.

Pickles sleeps with
the **covers** over his head.

crack cracks, cracked, cracking

The bathtub **cracked** when Big Hilda got into it.
The water is flowing through a **crack**
under the door.

crash crashes, crashed, crashing

Dingo **crashed** into a train.

creep creeps, crept, creeping

Babykins is **creeping** across the floor.
He is going to crawl into Father's lap.

cross

Nurse Nora has a red **cross** on her cap.
She is **cross** with her patient
because he won't stay in bed.

cross crosses, crossed, crossing

Dingo stopped his car at the **cross**ing
to let the children **cross** the street.
Very good, Dingo!

crush crushes, crushed, crushing

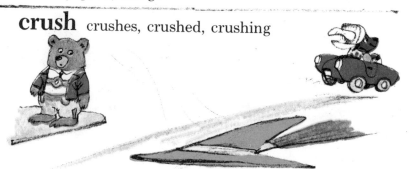

The wind blew Pappa Bear's hat into the street.
It was **crushed** by Dingo's car.

cry cries, cried, crying

The piglets are **crying** again.
Just look at all those tears!

cut cuts, cut, cutting

Father Cat bought a new tie.
Grandma said it was too long.
She **cut** off a piece to make it shorter.
Oh, Grandma! You didn't have to **cut** it *that* short!

Dd *Dd*

dandy!

dance
dances, danced, dancing
dancer

Ali Cat is **dancing** with Squeaky.
They are good **dancers**.

danger
dangerous

DANGER

Slow down, Dingo!
See that **danger** sign ahead.
You are driving at a very **dangerous** speed.

dark darkness

It is **dark** at night.
Blinky has a torch so that
he can see in the **darkness**.
He is not afraid of the **dark**.

Sunday
Monday
Tuesday
Wednesday
Thursday
Friday
Saturday

day daytime

Ali Cat is teaching Squeaky about **days**.
A **day** is one **daytime** and one night-time.
A **day** has a morning, a noon, an afternoon,
an evening, and a night.
There are seven **days** in a week.
Can you write them, Squeaky?
Very good, Squeaky.

dear

Dear Andy

Bumbles is writing a letter.
Oh **dear**! What a pity!
He will have to start all over again.

decide decides, decided, deciding

Fingers is eating ice cream.
He can't **decide** which spoonful to eat first.

deliver delivers, delivered, delivering

GoGo is **delivering** a package to Badger.
Something is leaking in that package, GoGo!

different

The piglets are alike. They all look the same.
Turkle and Macintosh are **different.**
They don't look at all alike.

destroy destroys, destroyed, destroying

Bully **destroyed** Babykin's sand castle.
That nasty ruffian ruined it.

dig digs, dug, digging

Huckle was **digging** a hole in the ground.
He **dug** so hard he got a hole in his trousers.

dining room

Pickles thought he was ready
to eat in the **dining room.**
He is not ready, is he?
Do what you should always do
before you eat, Pickles!

SUPER PICKLE !!!

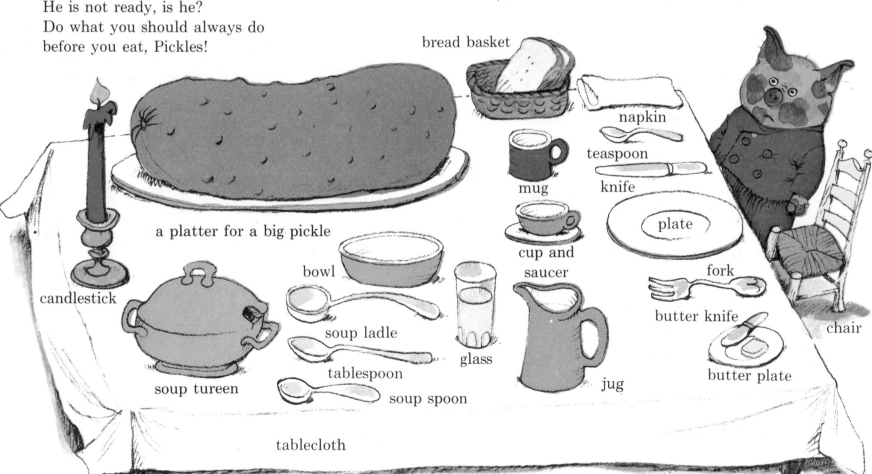

bread basket

napkin

teaspoon

knife

mug

plate

a platter for a big pickle

cup and
saucer

fork

candlestick

bowl

butter knife

chair

soup ladle

glass

soup tureen

tablespoon

jug

butter plate

soup spoon

tablecloth

dip dips, dipped, dipping

Bilgy took a **dip** in the ocean by accident.
Captain Fishhead **dipped** him out.

direction

Ali Cat was painting a **direction** sign
to show drivers the way to go.
Dingo knocked the sign down and
didn't know which **direction** to go.
Ali gave him **directions**. He told him where to go.

dirt dirty

Ozzie is playing in the **dirt**.
My, he is **dirty**!

distance

Baron von Crow ran out of petrol
and had to land a long **distance** from the airport.

dive dives, dived, diving

Annie fell into a bowl of soup.
Superbee **dived** in to save her.

divide divides, divided, dividing

Mamma Bear **divided** the pie into three pieces.

do does, did, done, doing

Squigley said, "How do you **do**?
Do you want your chimney cleaned?
I can **do** it and not get your house sooty."
See what Squigley has **done**!

doctor

Nurse Nora gives **Doctor** Pill a jab in the arm.
He must have the jab so that he will stay well.
A **doctor** can't take care of sick children if he is sick.

down

Spuds climbed up the ladder and slid **down** the slide.
Nice slide, Spuds!

draw draws, drew, drawn, drawing

The piglets put Pa Pig's hats on and Ali Cat **drew** faces on their tummies. What a funny place to **draw**!

dress dresses, dressed, dressing

Wiggles **dressed** himself.
He put on his coat
and trousers.
My! What a way
to get **dressed.**

drink drinks, drank, drunk. drinking

Pickles likes to **drink** milk.
He is **drinking** a big **drink**, isn't he?

drip drips, dripped
dripping

The tap was **dripping** tiny drops of water.
Mr. Fixit fixed it so that it would not **drip** at all.

drive drives, drove, driven, driving
driver

Dingo went for a **drive.**
He **drove** through HeeHaw's cornfield.
Dingo, you're a bad **driver.**

drop drops, dropped, dropping

When a **drop** of paint **dropped** on Ali Cat's nose, he **dropped** his paint can.

dry dries, dried, drying

Wiggles wears his raincoat to stay **dry**.
Flossie **dries** the dishes.

dump dumps, dumped, dumping

Whiff **dumped** the rubbish at the **dump.**

during

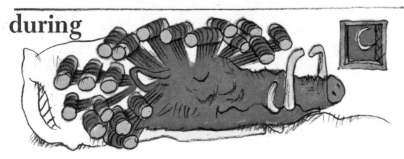

Brambles wears curlers in his hair **during** the night
so that it will look nice in the morning.

dust dusts, dusted, dusting

Flossie is **dusting** the house.
There is **dust** everywhere.

E e *E e*

extraordinary!

each

Each beggar has a tattered hat.
Every one of the beggars has a hat.

early

BOW WOW!

Doodledoo gets up **early** in the morning.
Henny gets up later.

earth

The sunflower is
growing in the **earth.**
Annie is sunbathing
on the sunflower.
The **earth** is the world
we all live on.
Ooch is an **earthworm**.

easy

It is **easy** for Andy
to eat from
the bottom of the jar.
It is not hard
for him to do.

eat eats, ate, eaten, eating

Pickles **eats** mustard on his hot dogs.

edge

Hilda is sitting on the **edge** of the chair.
Her soda is on the **edge** of the table.

either

Tom may have **either** a tuba or
a harmonica for a present.
He may have one or the other, not both.

else

Tom has a drum on his head.
He has something **else** on it, too.
He had better not play them now
or **else** Grandma will be angry.

empty empties, emptied, emptying

The barrel was full of treacle.
It was knocked over and now it is **empty**.
Take your tail out of the   Bumbles.

end ends, ended, ending

That was
a good story.

GoGo has come to the **end** of the book.
He has finished reading the story.
What is that on the **end** of his horn?

enjoy enjoys, enjoyed, enjoying

Blinky **enjoys** television. He really likes it.

enough

Pelican has had **enough**
fish for supper.
He doesn't need
or want any more.

enter enters, entered, entering

Squeaky **entered**
the cheese shop
to buy a piece of cheese.

39

entrance

Mamma Bear entered the bakery.
The beggars are standing at the **entrance**
waiting for her to come out.

envelope

Crabbie wrote a letter and put it in an **envelope**.

equal

Henny put an **equal** number of eggs
in each basket. Each holds the same number.

erase   erases, erased, erasing
eraser

Ali Cat is **erasing**
his drawing
with an **eraser**.

error

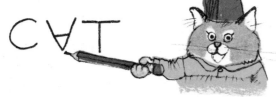

Ali Cat made an **error** in writing
the word "cat." He made a mistake.

even

Mamma Bear uses an **even** cup
of flour to make a cake.

See how level it is.
Even Babykins doesn't make that big a mess!

ever

Have you **ever** seen Squigley roller skate?
Squeaky never had—not before now.

every   everybody, everything

Every piglet had a cold and had to stay in bed.
They all had colds.
Everyone was very naughty.
Everything in the room was thrown **every**where.
Ma hopes **every**body will be well tomorrow.
She couldn't take this **every** day.

except

Keep the sunny side up!

Bow wow!

All of the chicks **except** one are singing nicely.

exchange exchanges, exchanged, exchanging

Mother Cat bought Father a hat the wrong size.
Father is taking it back so he can **exchange** it.

excite excites, excited, exciting

Bilgy is very **excited.**
He has caught a big fish.

excuse excuses, excused, excusing

Macintosh bumped into Big Hilda.
"Please **excuse** me," he said.
Big Hilda **excused** him.

exit

EXIT

When the film ended,

Huckle went out of the cinema by the side **exit.**

expect expects, expected, expecting

Mamma Bear is **expecting** company. She knows
company is coming. Here they come now, Mamma!

explode explodes, exploded, exploding

Mamma Bear's cake **exploded!**
What did you put in the cake, Mamma?

41

Ff

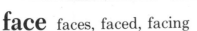
fantastic!

fair

Kitty always plays **fair**.
She shares her toys with her friends.

face faces, faced, facing

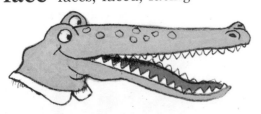

Smiley **faced** the clock.
He looked at the **face** of the clock
to see what time it was.
Why, someone has hung it upside down.

fair

Mamma Bear was in a cooking contest
at the country **fair**. She won last prize.

fact

Dingo is a terrible driver.
That is a **fact**. We know it is true.

fall falls, fell, fallen, falling

Squeaky **fell** asleep under a tree.
Bully tripped over him and had a nasty **fall**.
Then an apple **fell** on his head. Poor Bully!

family

Uncle and Aunty Cat and their children
visit the Cat **family**. Uncle Louie is
Mother Cat's brother. All belong to the same **family**.

Father Cat · Babykins · Grandma · Mother · Sister Kitty · Uncle Louie · Brother Tom · Aunty and all the cousins

42

farm

brook

meadow

haystacks

apple orchard

corn field

ploughed field

fence

lane

vegetable garden

stone wall

gate

barn

hayloft

water pump

farmhouse

woodpile

axe

barnyard

Farmer HeeHaw is working on his **farm.**
Company is coming to call on him.

well

rake

hoe

ladder

scythe

milk can

pitchfork

tractor

wagon

pail

farm truck

43

fascinate fascinates, fascinated, fascinating

Flossie is **fascinated** watching Big Hilda
dance a ballet. She can't stop looking at her.

fast

Dingo is driving too **fast**.
The sign tells him to go slow.
Stop going so **fast**, Dingo!

fat

Hilda is **fat**. Squigley is thin.
He is only **fat** after he has eaten a melon.

favour

Mother asks Kitty, "Please do me a **favour**.
Help me set the table. That would be nice."

feed feeds, fed, feeding

Babykins is **feeding** himself.
Put the food in your mouth, Babykins!
Do you hear me. . .in your MOUTH!!

feel feels, felt, feeling

Babykins has just had a bath.
He **feels** soft and cuddly.
Mother **feels** happy to have such a clean baby.

few

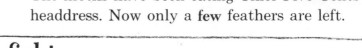

The moths have been eating Chief Five Cents'
headdress. Now only a **few** feathers are left.

fight fights, fought, fighting

Bully picked a **fight** with Fingers.
Let that be a lesson to you, Bully!

44

fill fills, filled, filling

Froggie **filled** his car with water.
Now he has a swimming pool
filled with children.

find finds, found, finding

HeeHaw lost his trousers.
He couldn't **find** them.
He **found** them sitting on the shelf.

finish finishes, finished, finishing

Tom has just **finished** building a tower.
I think he will start building a new one shortly.

fire

helmet fireman fire engine flames

leaky hose

The house is on **fire**! It is burning!
Turn your hose on the **fire** and put it out!
That is a brave **fireman.**

fish

not really?

no fooling!

The members of the Fishing Club
are eating **fish soup** and telling **fish** stories.
Stop floundering in the soup, Flounder!

fix fixes, fixed, fixing

Mr. Fixit is **fixing**
the broken clock.

45

flatten flattens, flattened, flattening
flat

A steam-roller **flattened** Dingo's car.
That is certainly a **flat** car!

float floats, floated, floating

Bilgy's boat is **floating**
on top of the water.

Hannibal's boat is sinking.

flow flows, flowed, flowing

Andy came in out of the rain.
When he took off his hat, a stream
of water **flowed** out of the brim.

flower

Pa Pig brought a bouquet of **flowers**
home to Ma Pig.

fly flies, flew, flown, flying

Baron von Crow **flew** into the railway tunnel.

fold folds, folded, folding

BOW WOW!

Crabbie is **folding** newspapers
to make paper hats.

follow follows, followed, following

Pa Pig **followed** Dingo into the mud hole.

food

Mother Cat went to the grocer's shop
to buy a loaf of bread.
Just look at all the **food** she brought home!
Oh, dear! She forgot to buy a loaf of bread!

ham

steak

jam

roast beef

pie

jelly

sausage

ice cream

cake

hamburger

mustard

raisins

bacon

frankfurters

soup

ketchup

prunes

cereal

buns

spaghetti

salami

butter

cheese

cocoa

peanut butter

milk

a dozen eggs

a pint of cream

salt

biscuits

foolish

Wiggles is being **foolish**.
He is acting in a silly way.

for

Haggis looked in the umbrella stand
for his bagpipes.
He played them **for** a long time.
For heaven's sake, STOP! Haggis,
for if you don't, Heather and Macintosh will leave.

forget forgets, forgot, forgotten, forgetting

Dingo backed his car out of the garage.
He **forgot** to open the door first.

free

Bully got a **free** apple.
It didn't cost him even a penny.

freeze freezes, froze, frozen, freezing

Do not stand in a pail of water
when it is **freezing** cold outside.
The water will **freeze** into ice.

fresh

Hmm, **fresh** gingerbread
is good to eat, but watch
out for **fresh** paint.

friend

friendly

Fingers and Ozzie are good **friends**.
Fingers gives Ozzie a **friendly** hug.

from

Ma Pig took one piglet
from the bathtub and hung him up to dry.
It is hard to tell one piglet
from another. They all look alike.

front

rear

walking forward

front

ahead

behind

under

The driver is at the **front** of the bus.
Haggis is at the back of the bus.
Annie is walking forward to the **front**
of the bus.

Pa Pig is sitting backwards,
facing the rear of the bus.
Father Cat is behind the bus.
Who is ahead of the bus? Who is under it?

fruit

Pickles loves to eat **fruit**.
When you eat a grape**fruit**, it should go
in your mouth—not anywhere else!

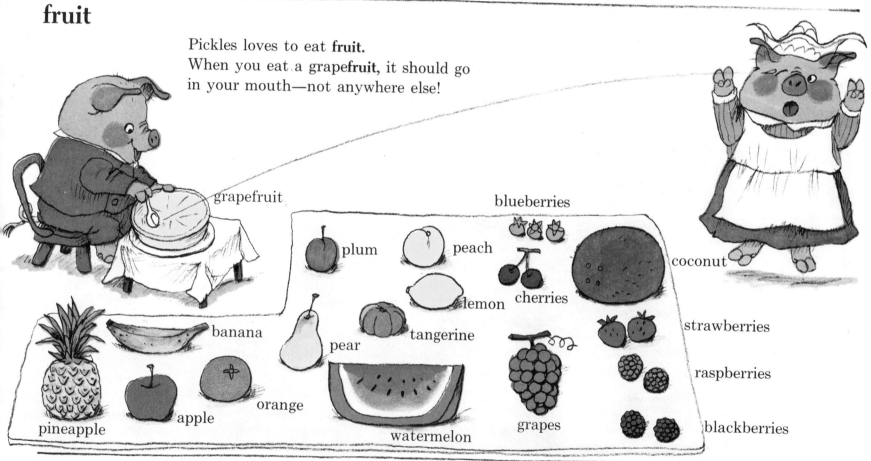

grapefruit

blueberries

plum

peach

coconut

lemon

cherries

banana

strawberries

pear

tangerine

raspberries

pineapple

apple

orange

watermelon

grapes

blackberries

full

Babykins was digging in the earth and found
some sparkling diamonds.
He filled a pail **full** of them and gave them
to his mother. She was **full** of joy, too.
Babykins kept one for himself.

Gg *Gg*

great!

garden

Daddy Bunny grows weeds in his **garden**.

game

The children are playing a **game** of tag.
Kitty is "it." Wiggles will be "it" next.

get gets, got, getting

When Father Cat
got off the train,
he **got** out his umbrella.
He forgot how to open it,
so he **got** wet.

garage

Mr. Fixit repairs cars in his **garage**.

garbage

Do you know what has four wheels and flies?
Of course! Whiff's **garbage** lorry.

Getting home, Mother Cat
showed him how to open an umbrella.
He **got** a good lesson in umbrella opening.
Father won't **get** wet again.

50

give gives, gave, given, giving

Father Cat **gave** Tom a gift on his birthday.
Tom's gift is **giving** Grandma a headache.

glad

I am happy

Superbee is **glad** that he can write.
He is happy he can.

glass

YOU ARE HANDSOME!

Brambles is admiring his hair in the **glass** mirror.
He is shaking hair tonic out of the **glass** bottle.
Careful, Brambles. Don't shake any
into your drinking **glass**.

glasses

Grandma can see better when she wears **glasses**.

go goes, went, gone, going

Dingo started the engine to make the car **go**.
He is **going** for a drive.

He **went** through a stop light. He was **going** too fast!

He **went** off the road.
His car will have to **go**
to the **garage** again.

good better, best

Babykins is a **good** boy.
He is wearing his **best** clothes.
He likes chocolate ice cream **better** than vanilla.

51

good-bye

Captain Fishhead dropped his watch in the water. **Good-bye,** watch!

grab grabs, grabbed, grabbing

The wind blew Heather's hat off her head. She **grabbed** it.

grade

Miss Nelly teaches the first **grade** at school.
Miss Tilly is the second-**grade** teacher.

grass

GoGo is cutting the **grass.**
Look out, Gus!

great

Andy has a big nose,
but Hannibal has a **great** big nose.
Andy thinks he is a **great** dancer.

ground

HeeHaw is digging
potatoes out of the **ground.**

group groups, grouped, grouping

One bug is all alone.
The other bugs
are in a **group.**
They are **grouped**
around the swimming pool.

grow grows, grew, grown, growing

Haggis **grows** vegetables in his garden.
Macintosh eats them so he will **grow** bigger.

Hh

he is a happy bee!

half halves

Chips had one whole bed. Mose didn't have a bed.
Chips sawed his bed in **half**.
Now they each have one of the **halves**.

handle

Mother Cat holds the cocoa pot by the **handle**.

hang hangs, hung, hanging

coat hanger

Wiggles forgot to **hang** his coat on the hook.
His mother **hung** it up for him on a coat **hanger**.

happen happens, happened, happening

Something **happened** to Mummy Bunny's fur coat.
The moths ate most of it.

happy

BOW WOW!

Doodledoo and Henny are very **happy** parents.
They have such a nice family of baby chicks.

hard

Dingo drove off the **hard** concrete road
into the soft mud. Mr. Fixit is trying
hard to pull him out.

have has, had, having

Baron von Crow **has**
an aircraft. It was
having trouble
and he **had** to jump out.
Look! He **has** on his
parachute *upside down!*
Have you ever seen such a sight?

53

head

Mose is at the **head** of the line—at the very front.
He has a **head** of cabbage on his **head.**
Smiley is at the tail end of the line.

health

Blinky is in good **health.** He feels fine.
Turkle's **health** is not so good. He is sick.

hear hears, heard, hearing

Grandma has never **heard**
such noise.

heat heats, heated, heating

Mamma is **heating** some soup for lunch.
It is time to turn off the **heat,** Mamma.

heavy heavier, heaviest

Pickles is **heavy.** He weighs a lot.
Macintosh says Pickles is **heavier** than he is.
Big Hilda is by far the **heaviest.**

help helps, helped, helping
helper

Babykins is **helping** Father Cat
make a mess of the living room.
They are Mother Cat's little **helpers.**

here

Mrs. Fishhead said, "Come **here!**
Supper is ready!"
Captain Fishhead called, "I can't.
I'm stranded out **here** on a rock."

54

hide hides, hid, hidden, hiding

Babykins is **hiding** from Father Cat.
Father is looking for him.

high

Baron von Crow is flying **high** in the sky.
Fly your plane properly, Baron.

hit hits, hit, hitting

Dingo **hit** an egg van.
It was a direct **hit**.

hold holds, held, holding

Mamma Bear is **holding** a pot.
The pot **holds** cocoa.
The pot has a leak.

hole

Haggis has a **hole** in his roof.
He never **mended** it because
on rainy days it is too wet to work.
And on sunny days it doesn't need **mending**.

hollow

Squigley is sleeping in a **hollow** log.
Don't wear your shoe in bed, Squigley.

honest

Macintosh is **honest**.
He always tells the truth.
He never tells lies.

honk honks, honked, honking

HONK! HONK! HONK!
Dingo likes to **honk** his horn.

hook

Wiggles forgot to hang his clothes on the **hook.**

hop hops, hopped, hopping

Gus **hopped** onto HeeHaw's nose.

horn

GoGo has three **horns.**
He blows one.
He hangs his hat and coat on the others.

horrid

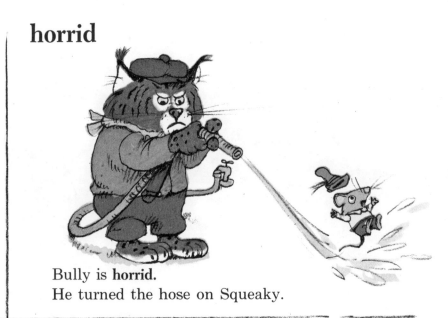

Bully is **horrid.**
He turned the hose on Squeaky.

hot hotter, hottest

It is a **hot** day.
Maud has never been **hotter.**
Molly says it is the **hottest** day of the year.

hour

There are 24 **hours** in every day.
Some **hours** are for playing.
During some **hours** we eat.
The night **hours** are for sleeping.

56

house

This is the Bunny family's **house.** It is a quiet Sunday at the Bunnys' **house.**
Mummy is cleaning out the attic.
She is throwing out things they don't need any more.

roof

chimney

attic window

shower

bedroom

cupboard

bathtub

bed

bathroom

lamp

wall

bureau

chair

stairs

floor

rug

living room

sofa

hall

bookcase

telephone

door

lawn

doorstep

pavement

how

Pickles knows **how** to eat cake. He uses his mouth.
How much did he eat? All of it?
How do you feel, Pickles?

however

Andy told Chips that he was building
the house upside down.
However, Chips paid no attention to Andy
and kept on building it that way.

hug hugs, hugged, hugging

Maud likes Brambles.
She **hugs** him and gives him a big kiss.

hungry hungrier, hungriest

The beggars are **hungry**.
They have never been **hungrier**.
They are **hungrily** eating their hats.

hunt hunts, hunted, hunting

Grandma lost her glasses.
Tom helps her **hunt** for them.
Wherever can they be?

hurry hurries, hurried, hurrying

Whiff is **hurrying** to the fire station. **Hurry**, Whiff!

hurt hurts, hurt, hurting

The door slammed on Smiley's tail
and **hurt** it. It **hurts!**
He is kissing it to make it better.

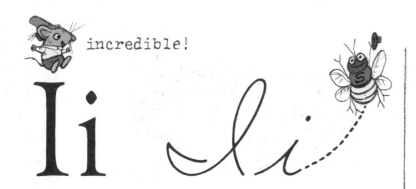
incredible!

Ii Ii

I me, my, mine, myself

Me, Myself, and I

I am SUPERBEE!!!!
I am TERRIFIC!!!!
I can write, "**ME, MYSELF,** and **I**"
in the sky. Watch **ME**!!!!!

ice

DANGER
THIN ICE

Big Hilda is skating on the **ice**.

if

Hannibal stuck his trunk out of the window
to see **if** it was raining. It was.
He will go out **if** the rain stops soon.

ill

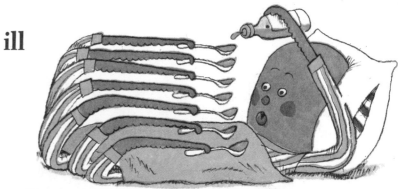

Fingers is **ill**. He is sick.
He is taking medicine to help him get well.

imp

Babykins is an **imp**.
He is mischievous.

important

How do you do?

Ouch!

It is **important** that we have good manners.
It matters a great deal to everyone.

ink

Ali Cat draws pictures with a pen and a bottle of **ink**.
It is important to put the **ink**
on the paper—not anywhere else.

insect

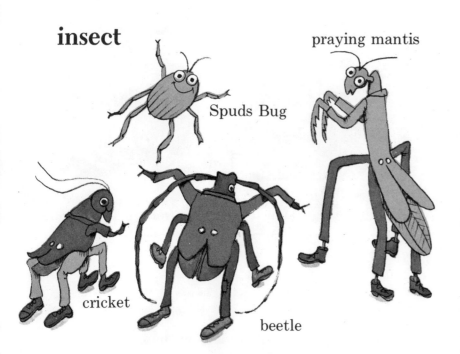

praying mantis

Spuds Bug

cricket

beetle

How would you like to be an **insect**
and have to put on so many shoes each morning?

inside

TELEPHONE

Big Hilda is stuck **inside** the phone booth.
She is telephoning someone to come
and help get her out.

instead

Bow wow!

Henny told her chick to say, "Peep peep."
Her chick said, "BOW WOW," **instead.**

into

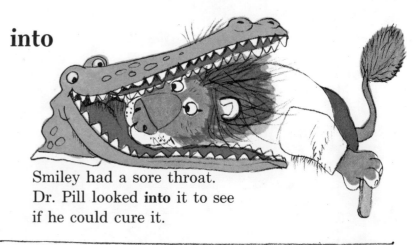

Smiley had a sore throat.
Dr. Pill looked **into** it to see
if he could cure it.

iron   irons, ironed, ironing

Mummy Bunny was **ironing** Daddy's shirt
with an **iron.** The doorbell rang.
The **iron** is still **ironing** Daddy's shirt.

it   its, itself

Dingo parked his car.
He left **its** motor running.
It drove off by **itself.**

itch   itches, itched, itching

Squigley's back is **itching.**
He is scratching it.

Jj *Jj*

a joy to watch!

jewellery

Mummy Bunny likes **jewellery.** She has a box
filled with rings, pins, and necklaces.
Sometimes Mummy lets Flossie wear them.

join *joins, joined, joining*

Hannibal was swimming.
Fingers **joined** him.
They swam together.

joy

my son!

Babykins brings much **joy** to his father.

jump *jumps, jumped, jumping*

HeeHaw **jumped** onto his tractor.

just

Doodledoo has **just** come out of the shoe shop
where he bought new shoes.
They fit **just** right.

Kk *Kk*

keen!

keep *keeps, kept, keeping*

Pappa Bear gave Mamma Bear
a new vacuum cleaner to **keep.**
It is to help her **keep** the house clean.
But it **keeps** running up the walls.

61

key

keyhole

Get out of the **keyhole**, Annie,
so that Turkle can put his **key** in it.

kick kicks, kicked, kicking

There was a stone in the bag Bully **kicked**.
He won't **kick** again soon with that foot.

kind

Flossie is very **kind.** When Grandma Cat
was sick she brought her a gift.
Grandma received many different **kinds** of gifts.

king

The **king** gave the queen a gold bracelet.
The queen gave the **king** a kiss.

62

kitchen

Mamma Bear has gone shopping.
The three beggars are making
a cake in her **kitchen.**
They are going to surprise her
with it when she returns.
She really will be surprised
when she returns, won't she?
What is that behind
the refrigerator door?

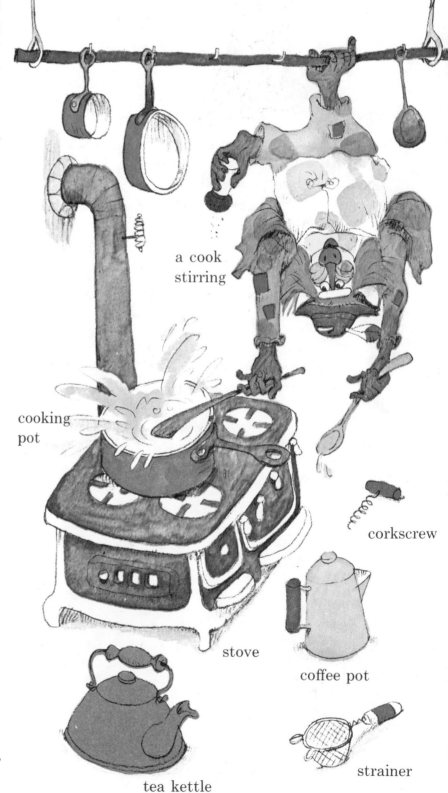

a cook
stirring

cooking
pot

corkscrew

stove

coffee pot

tea kettle

strainer

spice cabinet

Mamma returning home

cuckoo clock

refrigerator

tea pot

counter

clothes-washer

sink

dishwasher

delivery boy

freezer

mop and pail

frying pan

saucepan

lid

muffin pan

soup ladle

roasting pan

spilled ketchup

egg beater

cake pan

jug

funnel

cook book

potato peeler

a cook beating

mixing bowl

mustard jar

flour canister

tin opener

biscuit jar

potato masher

measuring jug

biscuit cutter

rolling pin

measuring spoons

shears

double boiler

pepper mill

spatula

blender

iron

colander

toaster

salt shaker

food grinder

knight

Knights wear armour.
They are very brave.

knock knocks, knocked, knocking

Mose **knocked** on the door.
Do not **knock** so hard, Mose.

knot

Squigley tied a **knot.**
Can you untie that nice **knot,** Squigley?

know knows, knew, known, knowing

Tom **knows** Haggis.
They **know** each other.
They both **know** how to make loud music.

lovely!

Ll Ll

lace laces, laced, lacing

Hooligan was **lacing** his shoes.
His shoe**lace** broke.
Hepzibah put a **lace** tablecloth on the table.

land lands, landed, landing

HeeHaw grows all kinds of food
on his **land.** That crazy Baron von Crow
just **landed** on his barn.

lap

Mother is trying to hold Babykins on her **lap.**
What a wriggler he is.

large

Fishhead caught a small fish. Bilgy caught a **large** one.

last lasts, lasted, lasting

Andy was the **last** one to get on the bus and had to sit on top. He is wondering how long the rain will **last.**

late

Bumbles was **late** for school.
He didn't get there on time.

laugh laughs, laughed, laughing

Maud told Molly something funny.
They are both **laughing** and giggling.

laundry

Baron von Crow flew into Big Hilda's **laundry,** which was hanging out to dry.

lay lays, laid, laying

Chips **laid** his cap on the table he had built.

That was not a very sturdy table, Chips. **Lay** it somewhere safe next time.

lazy

The beggars are a **lazy** bunch of loafers.
They just hang around doing nothing.

lead leads, led, leading
leader

The piglets went on a picnic and got lost.
"Follow the **leader**," says GoGo.
He **leads** them back to their family.

leak leaks, leaked, leaking

The water pipe is **leaking**.
Mr. Fixit is trying to stop the **leak**.

learn learns, learned, learning

Big Hilda is **learning** how to ride a bicycle.

leave leaves, left, leaving

Mamma Bear **left** the cake in the oven
too long. She is **leaving** the house.

left

left ⬅   ➡ right

Sneakers put a plimsoll on his **left** foot.
His right foot is bare.

length

Andy has a nose of great **length**.
Annie Ant ran along the **length** of it.

less

Six chicks were playing with blocks.
One chick went away to dig for bones.
There is one **less** chick playing with blocks.

let lets, let, letting

tick
tock

Father Cat **lets** Babykins play with his watch.
He allows him to play with it.
Foolish Father!

66

letter

Ali Cat says, "Words are made with **letters**."
Some **letters** are big.
Some are small.
All the **letters**
of the alphabet
are at the front of the book.

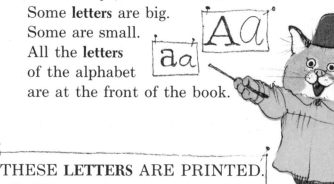

THESE **LETTERS** ARE PRINTED.

These letters are written

Squeaky is learning to write and print the different **letters**. What **letters** can you write or print?

letter

Squeaky wrote a **letter** to the Man in the Moon.
He asked him if he was made of cheese.
What do you think?

librarian

Miss Page is the **librarian** at the library.
She is helping Flossie find a book to read.
What is your **librarian's** name?

library

Little Chick is borrowing
a book at the **library**
to take home and read.

lie

I did!

When Mamma Bear asked Huckle
who watered her flower plants,
he told her the truth.
He would never tell a **lie**.
No good girl or boy ever does.

lie lies, lay, lain, lying

Big Hilda was so sleepy, she decided to **lie** down.
She **lay** asleep a long time.

67

lift lifts, lifted, lifting

Heather asked Macintosh if he would **lift** her chair and carry it into the next room. Macintosh **lifted** Heather too.

light lights, lighted or lit, lighting

The sun gives **light** in the daytime.
At night, when it gets dark,
Mother turns the **lights** on.
Father has **lit** a fire.
It throws a cheery **light.**

light

Pappa Bear's suitcase was heavy but Huckle's was **light.**

like likes, liked, liking

Maud and Molly **like** their new hats.
Maud's hat is just **like** Molly's.
It is just the same.

line lines, lined, lining

There is a **line** of people waiting for the bus.
Ali Cat is painting a **line**
down the middle of the street.

liquid

Water is a **liquid.** It pours.
When it freezes it turns into a solid.
Then it is hard.

listen listens, listened, listening

Daddy isn't **listening** to what Mummy
is telling him to do.
Listen to what Mummy has to say, Daddy.

little

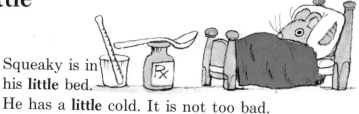

Squeaky is in
his **little** bed.
He has a **little** cold. It is not too bad.

live lives, lived, living

Doodledoo **lives** in a nice house.
He sells eggs for a **living.**
He has a good life.

long longer, longest

GoGo has **long** trousers on.
Mose's trousers are **longer.**

look looks, looked, looking

Wiggles is **looking** in the cupboard.
He is **looking** for his trousers.
His room **looks** a mess.
It **looks** as if he will have to
straighten his room.

loose

Pappa Bear's trousers are too **loose,**
but his coat is too tight.
He opened the taxi door and the door came **loose.**

lose loses, lost, losing

Chief Five Cents **lost** all his arrows
in the woods. Then he got **lost** himself.
HeeHaw found him and showed him the way home.

loud

Doctor Pill stubbed his toe.
He made a **loud** roar.

love loves, loved, loving

Kitty **loves** Pickles.
She gives him a big kiss.

low

Baron von Crow flew his plane so **low**
it almost hit a house.

Mm*Mm*

magnificent!

machine

Mr. Fixit can fix
any kind of **machine**.

camera

sewing machine

electric fan

typewriter

mail mails, mailed, mailing

"I have some **mail** for you," the postman
tells Pickles. Someone had **mailed** him
a letter. . .and a pickle!

make makes, made, making

Chips is **making** a wagon.
He **makes** a lot of noise too.

many more, most

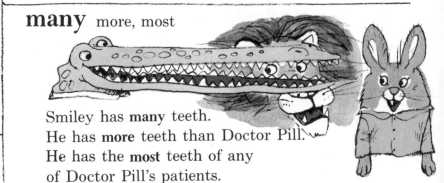

Smiley has **many** teeth.
He has **more** teeth than Doctor Pill.
He has the **most** teeth of any
of Doctor Pill's patients.

march marches, marched, marching

The band is **marching** down the street.
Everybody loves a **march**.

70

mark marks, marked, marking

Fingers and Macintosh are playing a game.
They take turns making **marks** with their crayons.
Don't **mark** the wall, Macintosh.

match matches, matched, matching

The trousers and jacket of Father Cat's
new suit **match**. They are of the same colour
and material.
He is very careful when he lights
a fire with a flaming **match**.

may might

Bilgy **may** have caught a big fish.
He is pulling with all his **might**.
May we see what you have caught, Bilgy?
Too bad. Keep trying.
You **might** catch a fish next time.

meal

Pickles eats three **meals** every day.
In the morning he eats breakfast.
At **noon** he eats lunch.
In the evening he eats supper.
If lunch or supper is a big, big, **meal**
it is called dinner.
Eat your dinner, Pickles!

measure measures, measured, measuring

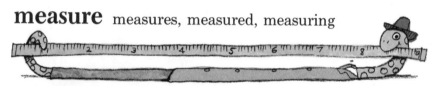

Squigley is **measuring** himself with
a tape **measure** to see how long he is.

medicine

Nurse Nora gives Doctor Pill his **medicine**.
Soon he will feel much better.

meet meets, met, meeting

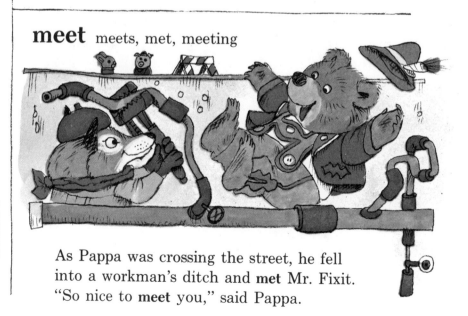

As Pappa was crossing the street, he fell
into a workman's ditch and **met** Mr. Fixit.
"So nice to **meet** you," said Pappa.

melt melts, melted, melting

Mamma Bear put the ice cream on the stove
instead of in the refrigerator.
The ice cream **melted.**

mend mends, mended, mending

Tom tore his trousers.
Grandma is
mending them.

mess

Babykins has made a **mess.**

middle

He is sitting
in the **middle** of
Mother's new rug.

mind minds, minded, minding

Kitty is **minding** Babykins.
He is not behaving.
He won't **mind** her.
Kitty doesn't **mind** if he gets cereal
all over his face, but she does **mind**
his getting it all over the rug.
Naughty boy!

minute

Chips will finish chopping down the tree
in a **minute.** He will be finished
in a tiny bit more time.

mischief

Babykins tickled Father's nose
while he was reading a magazine.
He is always up to some **mischief!**

miss misses, missed, missing

Father Cat **missed** the boat.
He was too late to get on before it sailed.
Wiggles lost a tooth.
It is **missing.**

mistake

Mamma Bear asked Huckle
to water her flower so that it would grow.
Someone has made a **mistake.**
Water won't make flour grow!

mix mixes, mixed, mixing

Mrs. Fishhead is **mixing** things together
to make a nice stew. She is all **mixed** up.
She should put in the sand and sea shells
before she puts in the seaweed.

money

Kitty bought a doll with the **money**
she earned for baby-sitting with Babykins.

month

Ali Cat is teaching Squeaky the names
of the **months**. There are 12 **months** in a year.
In what **month** is your birthday?

JANUARY FEBRUARY MARCH	APRIL MAY JUNE	JULY AUGUST SEPTEMBER	OCTOBER NOVEMBER DECEMBER

moon

The **moon** is shining brightly.
Baron von Crow can see where
he is going in the **moon**light.

move moves, moved, moving

Dingo's car was stuck. It couldn't **move.**
No one else could **move** because of him.
Macintosh **moved** Dingo's car out of the way.

much more, most

The beggars are eating Mamma Bear's jam.
"Hmmm, I feel **much** better," says Wolfson.
"Is there **more**?" asks HaHaHa.
"**Most** of it is on your face," says Baboody.

must

Blinky **must** close the door if he wants
to stop the snow from coming in.

music musical, musician

double bass

violin

triangle

trumpet

cymbals

THE CATS' MEOWERS

piano

clarinet

drum

bugle

tuba

banjo

saxophone

guitar

Tom likes to play **music**
on his **musical** instruments.
He is a fine **musician**. Grandma likes to sing songs
to Tom's **music**. Together they have a good orchestra.

nifty!

Nn *Nn*

name names, named, naming

The **name** of the frog is "Froggie."
Froggie is what he is called.
He is falling off a piece of wood **named** a "log."

nap

napkin

Pa Pig ate too much for lunch.
He was sleepy so he lay down and took a **nap**.
He forgot to take off his **napkin**.

narrow

wide   narrow

The doorway is not wide enough for big Hilda to get through. It is too **narrow** for her.

naughty

Babykins doesn't mean to be **naughty**.
He just can't seem to help it.

near

nearly

The beggars are **near** the table.
They are close by.
It is **nearly** lunchtime.
Mamma **nearly** forgot she had a cake baking.
It's a good thing the oven is **near**.

neat

Flossie is **neat**. She is tidy.
Wiggles is not very **neat**. He is untidy.

need

needs, needed, needing

Brambles **needs** a haircut. The barber **needs** a new comb. He **needs** a haircut, too.

neighbour

Ooch Worm has a new **neighbour.**
It is Spuds, who just moved into the next house.

neither

Neither of the bunnies is behaving well—not one bunny nor the other.
Neither of the teachers wants her pupils to misbehave.

75

never

Ali Cat says, "**Never! Never! Never**
play with matches. It would make us
very sad if you got a bad burn."

new

Pappa Bear bought three **new** suits.
Mamma Bear couldn't *bear* seeing
the beggars in their old rags.
So she gave the **new** suits to them.

news

Mummy told Daddy some good **news**.
She told him something he didn't know.
He was so happy about the good **news**,
he gave her a big kiss.

next

Ozzie was sitting **next** to Hannibal
in Doctor Pill's waiting room.
Nurse Nora asked them whose turn
it was **next** to see the doctor.

nice

Mother is giving Babykins
a **nice** kiss before he goes to sleep.
He is a very **nice** and good baby
when he is asleep.

no

Sneakers got dressed.
He forgot to put on his trousers.
He has **no** trousers on.
No, Sneakers. You cannot
go out dressed like that.
Put on your trousers this instant!

noise

Who is making all that **noise** upstairs
when he should be quiet and sleeping?

none

Two piglets have hats.
One piglet has **none.**
He hopes someone will give him one.

not

Bilgy is fishing while sitting in the boat.
Captain Fishhead is fishing
but he is **not** sitting in the boat.

note

Sneakers wrote a **note** on a piece of paper.
He folded it and sent it to Bumbles.

nothing

Mamma Bear gave the beggars a bowl
of peanut-butter. They ate it all.
There is **nothing** left.
They even ate the bowl.

now

Dingo must stop right **now!**
Right this minute!

number

Ali is teaching Squeaky about **numbers.**
Now, repeat after Ali

1, one
2, two
3, three
4, four
5, five
6, six
7, seven
8, eight
9, nine
10, ten

oh look!

O o O o

obey obeys, obeyed, obeying

Mamma told Huckle to take his muddy feet out of the house. He is **obeying** her. He will do it.

object

Heather threw an **object** out the window. The thing almost hit Haggis.

of

Huckle is eating from a jar **of** honey. Honey is made **of** flower nectar.

off

Macintosh took his clothes **off**. He left his hat on. He turned the water on.

From a long way **off** he heard Haggis shouting, "Turn **off** the water, Macintosh!"

offer offers, offered, offering

Mr. Fixit was trying to straighten the bend in the tricycle. Chips **offered** to help him. Mr. Fixit did not accept Chip's **offer**.

often

Squigley **often** eats several melons at a time. He does it frequently.

oil oils, oiled, oiling

Dingo is **oiling** his car.
The **oil** keeps the car from squeaking.

one

Someone gave the beggars a bicycle.
They have **one** bike for the three of them.
The **one** who fell off will have to swim.

old

Gramps is very **old**.
He is not young any more.
He has an **old**-fashioned car.
It is 50 years **old**.

only

Chief Five Cents broke his one and **only** bow.
If **only** he hadn't pulled so hard!

on

Tom turned **on** the vacuum cleaner.

open opens, opened, opening

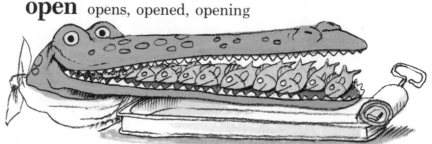

Smiley **opened** a can of sardines. He put them in his
open mouth. Shut your mouth, Smiley!

once

Tom was **once** at Macintosh's house.
He was there only one time—just **once**.
They had bones for supper and Tom ate one.
Once was enough! He will never eat another bone.

order orders, ordered, ordering

Mummy **ordered** Wiggles to put his room in **order**.
He put everything in its right place.
Good boy!

other

Brambles is making himself handsome. He has hair tonic in one hoof and a powder puff in the **other**.

out

Blinky was going **out** to play.
The door was **out** of order.
It wouldn't open, so he went **out** of the window.

outside

Mr. Fixit is working inside the house.
Chips is working **outside** the house.
Ali Cat is painting the **outside** of the house.

over

The sun was shining **over**head.
Macintosh was walking **over** the bridge.
Bully pushed him **over** into the dirt.
Macintosh threw Bully **over** the side.
Bully went under! Good for you, Macintosh!

own owns, owned, owning

Mose **owns** a canoe.
It belongs to him.
He is singing a happy song
as he paddles his very **own**
canoe down the stream.

80

P p

perfect!

paint paints, painted, painting

Ali Cat is **painting** a picture.
He is using many different colours of **paint**.
Do you **paint** pictures?

pack packs, packed, packing

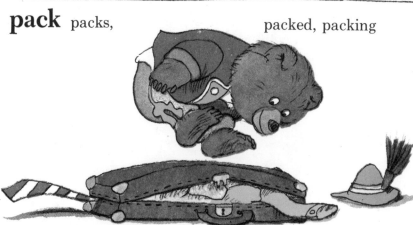

Pappa Bear is going on a trip. He is **packing** his bag.

pair

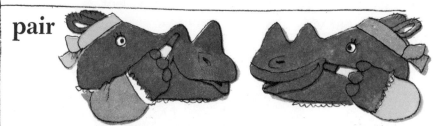

Any two things that are alike are a **pair**.
Now here is a **pair** of silly girls.
Each girl has a **pair** of ears.
They each have two ears.

package

Bumbles wrapped some things in a **package**.
Oh dear! He has wrapped his **foot**, too!

paper

Ali Cat is tearing a piece of old news**paper**.
Pages in books are made of **paper**.
Be careful that you don't tear them.

page

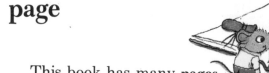

This book has many **pages**.

pain

Pickles ate too many green apples.
Now he has a **pain** in his stomach.

park parks, parked, parking

Dingo went to the zoo in the **park**.
There was no place to **park** his car
in the **parking** space.
Look where he **parked** it! Oh, that Dingo!

81

part

Babykins is eating a biscuit. **Part** of it is in his mouth. **Part** is in his paw, and **part** of it is on Father's new suit.

partner

Big Hilda has Macintosh for a dancing **partner**.

party

Andy blew out all the candles at his birthday **party**.

pass passes, passed, passing

When Dingo **passed** a red light,
a policeman **passed** him a copy of the Highway Code.

past

Sneakers walked **past** Mose,
who was shovelling snow. He walked right by him.

paste pastes, pasted, pasting

Bumbles has a new jar of **paste**. He was **pasting** pictures in a scrapbook. He **pasted** his paws together.

patch patches, patched, patching

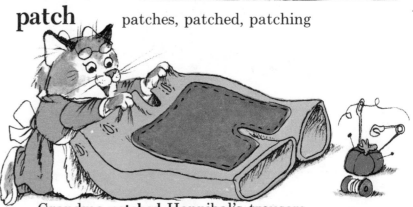

Grandma **patched** Hannibal's trousers.
That is a big **patch**, Grandma.

pay pays, paid, paying

Mother Cat **pays** money for the groceries.

Babykins is **paying** attention
to Spuds, who is dancing a jig.

pen
pencil

Ali Cat's **pen** leaks.

He will have to write with his **pencil**.

perhaps

It is very windy out.

Perhaps Hooligan should have stayed inside.

Maybe he should have.

phonograph

Bumbles put a record on the **phonograph**.

A **phonograph** is also called a record player.

The record will start to turn, around and around.

photograph

Whiff is taking a **photograph** of his dust lorry.

He is taking a picture of it with his camera.

pick picks, picked, picking

Mother **picked** flowers in the garden.

Then she **picked** out her very nicest vase to put them in.

Now Babykins is **picking** up the vase.

Be careful of that nice vase, Babykins!

piece

Pickles ate a **piece** of pie.

He didn't eat the whole of it.

He left a **piece**. That is *some* **piece**!

83

pin

Babykins needs **pins**
to keep his nappy on.

pipe

Mr. Fixit is having a hard time
stopping the leak in the water **pipe**.
His smoking **pipe** floats.

place places, placed, placing

Tom and Kitty sat in their **places** at the table.
Mother **placed** the cake on the table.
Squeaky! Where are your manners?
That is no **place** to be sitting.

plain

Ali Cat took a **plain** piece of paper
and wrote his name in **plain,** simple letters.
You are holding the paper upside down, Ali.

plan plans, planned, planning

If Chips had **planned** before he started to build,
his house would have had windows. But he didn't
think ahead. Maybe next time you had better
draw some **plans,** Chips.

plant plants, planted, planting

HeeHaw is **planting** seeds in the ground.
My, those are fast-growing **plants!**

play plays, played, playing

Ozzie is watching Sneakers and
Bumbles **play** a game of Ring Toss.
Ozzie likes to **play** pirate.

please pleases, pleased, pleasing

please?

BEANS

Huckle says, **"Please,"** when he asks for something.
It **pleases** his mother that he has such good manners.

plenty

Mamma has **plenty** of pies.
She has more than enough for the beggars.

point points, pointed, pointing

Where is Hooligan **pointing**?
Why, he is **pointing** at the apples
that fell on the **points** of GoGo's horns.

policeman

POLICE

The **policeman** has captured a band
of robbers and is taking them to jail.

polite

Andy says, "Hello, Annie. How are you
feeling today?" He is very **polite**.
He is pleasant and kind to others.

poor

Chips, that was **poor** work you did
on the chair you made for Heather.

possible

It is **possible** for Maud and Molly
to put more make-up on their faces,
but it is not likely.

85

pound

Big Hilda weighed herself at the butcher's shop. She weighs eight hundred **pounds**.

pound pounds, pounded, pounding

Grandma **pounded** Bully on the head because he splashed mud on her dress.

pour pours, poured, pouring

Pickles is **pouring** syrup on his pancakes.

present

Dingo received a new car for a birthday **present**. At the **present** time it is nice and shiny.

present presents, presented, presenting

The policeman **presented** Dingo with a traffic warning. He gave it to him for speeding.

press presses, pressed, pressing

Pappa took his suit to the tailor shop to be **pressed**. The suit was put in a **press**. The tailor **pressed** the "on" button. . . . . .and the suit was **pressed**.

pretty prettier, prettiest

I am! I am!

Maud and Molly are arguing over who is **prettier**. You are both **pretty**, girls.

price

Daddy asked Mummy the **price** of her new hat.
He wanted to know how much money she paid.

print prints, printed, printing

Badger borrowed a book from the library. The pages
of the book are **printed** with words and pictures.
He left foot**prints** on the rug.

promise promises, promised, promising

Captain Fishhead **promised** to bring back
a fish for supper. He kept his **promise.**

protect protects, protected, protecting

Turkle is **protecting** some chicks.
He is keeping them from getting wet.

pull pulls, pulled, pulling

Babykins is **pulling** the tablecloth.

punish punishes, punished, punishing

Wiggles is **punishing**
his new trousers
for getting muddy.
He is spanking them.

push pushes, pushed, pushing

Huckle **pushed** the kitchen door open.

put puts, put, putting

Big Hilda fell asleep and
needed to be **put** to bed.
Macintosh is **putting** her there.

Qq 2q

quite clever!

quarrel quarrels, quarrelled, quarrelling

Hepzibah and Hooligan were **quarrelling**
over who was to use the bicycle.
It broke in two. That settled that **quarrel.**

quarter

Mamma Bear cut a pie into four equal parts.
Huckle ate one **quarter** and
the beggars ate the other three **quarters.**

question

Tom asked his mother a **question.**
The **question** was, "May I play outside?"
The answer to his **question** was, "No, you may not."

88

quick

Quick! Hurry! Turn off the stove!
The pot is boiling over.

quiet

It is **quiet** now. Grandma is sleeping.
When Babykins plays the tuba, it will be noisy.

quit quits, quitted, quitting

Bully was teasing Flossie.
Macintosh made him **quit.**
He made him stop at once.

quite

Bilgy's boat is full of fish.
That's **quite** a load of fish, Bilgy.

Rr

remarkable!

race races, raced, racing

Dingo and Baron von Crow are **racing**
to see who can go the fastest.
They are having a **race**.

radio

Mr. Fixit is fixing the **radio**.

rain rains, rained, raining

It is **raining**.
Gus and Annie are sitting
under a toadstool to keep dry.

raise raises, raised, raising

Bow wow!

A gentleman always **raises** his hat
when he meets a lady on the street.

rather

Babykins would **rather**
suck his toe than his
thumb. He prefers it.

reach reaches, reached, reaching

Fingers **reached** across the table for some **biscuits**
That is bad manners.
He should have asked Pickles to pass the plate.

read reads, read, reading

Mamma is **reading** a book.
It tells her how to be a good cook.
You are **reading** it upside down, Mamma.

ready

Ma Pig is **ready** to give the piglets
their baths—right now! Where did they go?

89

real

At HeeHaw's first **real** birthday party everyone played "Pin the Tail on the Donkey."
Soon HeeHaw had three paper tails and one **real** tail.

reason

What **reason** does Mr. Fixit have for wearing rubber boots? Why does he? The **reason** is that he doesn't want to get his feet wet.

remember   remembers, remembered, remembering

Captain Fishhead
stopped his boat.
He **remembered** to throw the anchor overboard.
But he forgot to let go of it.
Now he **remembers** he has his new suit on.
Too late, Captain.

remove   removes, removed, removing

Badger **removed** Froggie from the cement mix. Wash Froggie off quickly to **remove** all that cement. Nobody wants a cement frog.

repair   repairs, repaired, repairing

Mose's boots are worn out.
They are being **repaired.**

rest   rests, rested, resting

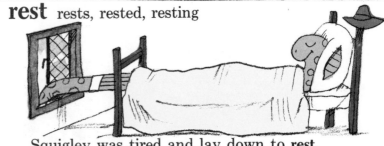

Squigley was tired and lay down to **rest.**
A part of him is **resting** on the bed,
but the **rest** of him is out of the window.

return   returns, returned, returning

Mrs. Fishhead bought a new hat.
Captain Fishhead made her **return** it
to the shop because it was too silly.
Soon she **returned** home with a sillier hat.

rich

Father Cat is very **rich.** He has just
about everything anyone could want.
He has a beautiful wife.
He has healthy children.
And he has Grandma who mends his socks.

ride rides, rode, ridden, riding

Doodledoo went for a **ride** with Dingo.
He is never going **riding** with him again.

right

Sneakers kicked the ball
with his **right** foot. He wanted to kick it
right to Bumbles—straight at him. But it didn't
go the **right** way. It went to the wrong place.

ring rings, rang, rung, ringing

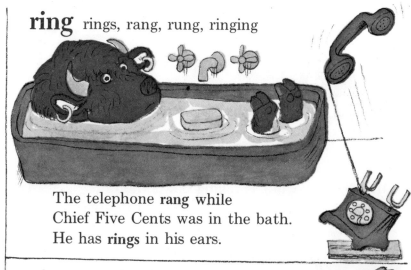

The telephone **rang** while
Chief Five Cents was in the bath.
He has **rings** in his ears.

ripe

Ripe melons are soft and ready to eat.
Big Hilda squeezed a melon to see if it was **ripe.**

rise rises, rose, risen, rising

Polite boys **rise** from their seats
when a lady enters the room.
One polite boy's balloon is **rising.**

rock rocks, rocked, rocking

Babykins put a **rock** in his cradle.
He is **rocking** it to sleep.

roll rolls, rolled, rolling

Just look at what is **rolling** down the hill!
A wheel, a ball, a **roll** of paper, and Squigley!

room

Mose had a party.
Annie was late and couldn't get in the **room**.
There was no more **room** for anyone.

rough

Doctor Pill is lying on the smooth beach.
Bilgy is on the **rough,** stormy sea.

round

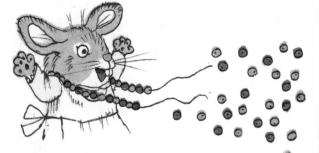

Mummy was wearing a string of **round** beads
round her neck.
Now there are beads all a**round**.

rub rubs, rubbed, rubbing

There was a stain on Pa Pig's coat. Ma Pig **rubbed**
and **rubbed** the stain with the stain remover.

rule

Ma Pig has a **rule** that Pickles must wash
his face and hands before eating. He must do it!

run runs, ran, running

Dingo **ran** his car into the **shop**.
The manager is **running** after him.

rush rushes, rushed, rushing

Father is **rushing** to catch a train.
He is in a great hurry.

S s

superb!

sack

Ma Pig is a good dressmaker.
She made a dress out of a flour **sack**.

sad

The piglets are **sad**.
They are crying.

safe

It is not **safe** to play in the street.
Always play on the **pavement** or in your **garden**.

sail sails, sailed, sailing

Bilgy is **sailing** his **yacht**.
The wind blows on the **sail** to make it go.

sale

Mamma took Pappa to a **sale**. It costs less money
to buy at the **sale** price than at the **usual** prices.

same

Pa Pig is wearing two ties.
They are both the **same**.
They are both **coloured** blue and green.

save saves, saved, saving

help!

Mrs. Fishhead **saves** pieces of string.
She keeps them to use when they are needed.
Spuds fell in the water. He couldn't swim.
Mrs. Fishhead threw him a string and **saved** him.

scrape scrapes, scraped, scraping

Pelican fell down and **scraped** his chin.

scratch scratches, scratched, scratching

Smiley has an itchy tail.
He is **scratching** it.

scribble scribbles, scribbled, scribbling

Babykins is **scribbling**.
He doesn't know
how to write, but he is trying.

scrub scrubs, scrubbed, scrubbing

Mamma **scrubbed** that pot too hard.

season

spring   summer   autumn   winter

There are four **seasons** in the year.
They are spring, summer, **autumn,** and winter.

seat seats, seated, seating

Mummy left her hat on the **seat** of the chair.
Hannibal is **seating** himself in the chair.

see sees, saw, seen, seeing

Grandma was sick in bed.
Doctor Pill came to **see** Grandma.
He wanted to **see** if she was feeling better.
What a sight he **saw**! Grandma was **better**!

seem seems, seemed, seeming

The beggars **seem** hungry.
They look hungry, don't they?

sell sells, sold, selling

Mummy sent Daddy to the shop to buy a broom.
The shopkeeper **sold** him a broom.
He is **selling** him a lot of other things, too.

serve serves, served, serving

Mamma **served** a big **serving** of soup to the beggars.

set sets, set, setting

Mother **set** the tablecloth on the television **set**.
Then she **set** Father's supper in front of him.
He is watching a football game.

sew sews, sewed, sewing

Grandma is **sewing** with a needle and thread.
She is making a new suit for Father.
Sew that sleeve a little shorter, Grandma.

shade

Gus is singing
in the **shade** of
a toadstool.

shadow

Squeaky is trying
to run away
from his **shadow**.

shake shakes, shook, shaken, shaking

Ozzie and Pelican **shake** feet when they meet.
Mummy is **shaking** dust out of her mop.

shall

"**Shall** I give you your medicine now?" Nurse Nora asks Doctor Pill. "If you must," says he.

shape

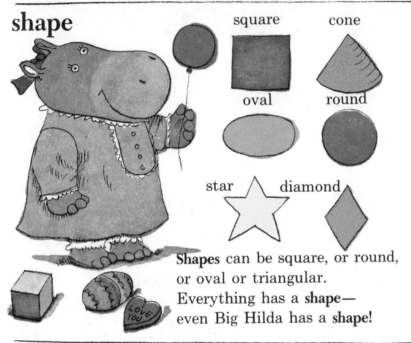

square

cone

oval

round

star

diamond

Shapes can be square, or round, or oval or triangular. Everything has a **shape**— even Big Hilda has a **shape**!

share shares, shared, sharing

The beggars found an old coat.
They decided to **share** it.
Wolfson got one piece.
Babooby got another piece.
HaHaHa got the buttons. Ha! Ha!

sharp

The butcher was cutting meat with a **sharp** knife.

she her, hers, herself

Kitty has a doll.
Her doll is sick.
She is taking care
of **her** doll
all by **herself.**

shell shells, shelled, shelling

Turkle and Crabbie have hard **shells** on their backs. They are **shelling** peas.

shine shines, shone, shining

Brambles put grease on his hair to make it **shine.**
The sun is **shining** on his **shiny** hair.

96

shiver shivers, shivered, shivering

Smiley is taking a cold shower. Brrrrrrrrr!
He is **shivering.** His teeth are chattering.

shop shops, shopped, shopping

Badger went **shopping** for a pair of sunglasses.
He tried on every pair in the **shop.**

should

HeeHaw **should** get new water pails. He needs them.

shout shouts, shouted, shouting

Grandma **shouted** at Tom to stop that noise.
My, she can really **shout** when she is angry.

show shows, showed, shown or showed, showing

Huckle **showed** Pickles where Mamma's cake
was baking. He pointed to where it was.

shut shuts, shut, shutting

Whiff came into the house and
forgot to **shut** the **doors.**

sick

Ozzie is **sick.** He is not feeling well.

side

Captain Fishhead dropped his watch
over the **side** of his boat.
Look on the other **side,** too, Fishhead.

97

sign

Ali Cat was painting a **sign**.
Now he is painting a window.

silence silences, silenced, silencing
silent

Bully was very noisy in the library.
Macintosh **silenced** him. Bully is **silent**.

sing sings, sang, sung, singing
singer
Gus is **singing** in the moonlight.
He is a good **singer**.

sink sinks, sank, sunk, sinking

Bilgy took Big Hilda for a boat ride.
Help! The boat is **sinking**.

sit sits, sat, sitting

Smiley is **sitting** on the chair.

size

Pappa Bear bought a new overcoat, but
it is the wrong **size**. It does not fit Pappa.

ski skis, skied, skiing

Badger **skied** down the hill on his **skis**.
He stopped at the bottom of the hill.

98

skip skips, skipped, skipping

Pa Pig told Big Hilda
to stop **skipping** on his pavement.

sky

Baron von Crow lost a wheel in the **sky**.

sleep sleeps, slept, sleeping

Chief Five Cents is **sleeping**.
He won't wake up.

slide slides, slid, sliding

Blinky is **sliding** on the smooth ice.

slip slips, slipped, slipping

HeeHaw **slipped** on a **slippery** banana skin.

slow slows, slowed, slowing

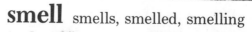

Dingo knows he must **slow** down where
children are playing. Go **slowly**, Dingo.

smell smells, smelled, smelling

Andy **smelled** supper burning in the kitchen.

smile smiles, smiled, smiling

Fingers always **smiles** when his picture is taken.
Look at his big grin.

smoke smokes, smoked, smoking

Smoke is coming out of Mamma's stove as usual.
Mr. Fixit is **smoking** a pipe while he mends the stove.

smooth

HeeHaw is pressing Pa Pig's suit to make
it **smooth.** The road is **smooth** except for
one rough place—just ahead of you, HeeHaw.

soft

Mrs. Fishhead squeezed the tomato
to see if it was hard or **soft.**
It was **soft.**

soil soils, soiled, soiling

Babykins has **soiled** another bib.
There is a big blob of food on it.
Mother will put it in the **soiled**-clothes basket.

solid

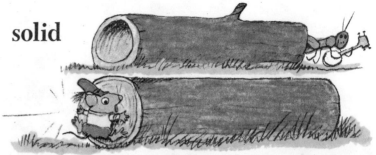

Gus ran through a hollow log.
Squeaky tried to run through a **solid** log.
You know that can't be done, Squeaky.

some
somehow
someone

Some beggars were standing on a bridge.
Some of them were very dirty,
but one was just plain filthy.
Someone drove across the bridge.
Somehow the beggars fell off it.
Not just **some** of them—all of them.

something

Ozzie ate **something** he shouldn't have.
What was the thing, Ozzie?

sometimes

Sometimes Ooch Worm will eat
only one rotten apple at a time,
but sometimes he will eat two.

somewhat

Froggie can leap somewhat farther than Gus.

somewhere

Little Chick is somewhere in Macintosh's kitchen.
I wonder where he can be?

soon

Baron von Crow will soon be all wet.
He will be wet in a very short time.

sort sorts, sorted, sorting

Heather is sorting out her dishes.
She is putting all the good dishes in one place
and all the cracked ones in another place.

sound

Grandma was sound asleep.
She was awakened by a loud sound.
Why, Babykins! Who taught you to play the tuba?

speak speaks, spoke, spoken, speaking

Badger is speaking to Spuds.
He is telling him he dropped something.

spell spells, spelled, spelling

Ooch Worm can spell
the word "love."

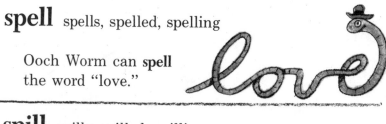

spill spills, spilled, spilling

Father spilled the milk.

101

splash splashes, splashed, splashing

Dingo drove through a mud puddle and **splashed** Bully. Serves Bully right.

squirm squirms, squirmed, squirming

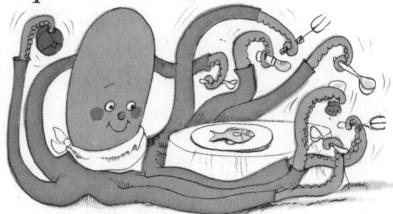

Fingers is wriggling. Stop **squirming**, Fingers!

spot

Ali Cat has **spots** of paint all over his jacket.

stamp stamps, stamped, stamping

Mommy tried to stick a **stamp** on a letter. It wouldn't stick. She was so angry she **stamped** her foot.

spring springs, sprang or sprung, springing

The fire alarm rang. The fireman **sprang** out of bed.

stand stands, stood, standing

Pickles is sitting. Wiggles is **standing**. They are eating at a hot-dog **stand**.

squash squashes, squashed, squashing

Big Hilda sat on a melon and **squashed** it.

star

At night Flossie likes to look at the **stars** in the sky.

start starts, started, starting

Dingo **started** his car.
He is **starting** to go for a drive.
Be careful! **Start** right now, Dingo!

stay stays, stayed, staying

Wiggles **stayed** in the barrel. Sneakers got out.

step steps, stepped, stepping

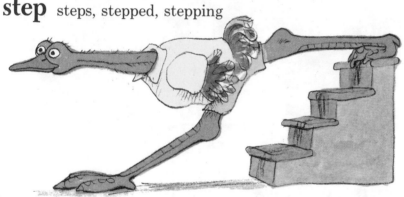

Ozzie **stepped** down the **steps**.

stick sticks, stuck, sticking

Pickles was **stuck** in the mud.
HeeHaw took a **stick** and
lifted him out. The mud
stuck to Pickles.

still

Father was lying very **still**.
Babykins jumped up and down
and **still** Father didn't move.

stop stops, stopped, stopping

The bus **stopped** at the bus **stop**.
Stop crying, children! **Stop!** I say.

store stores, stored, storing

Nutty Squirrel **stores** nuts
on the shelves
in his nut **store**.
He keeps them there
until they are sold.

story

Father read a **story**
to Babykins.
The **story** was about
three kittens.

straight

Ali Cat drew a curved line.
Now he is drawing a **straight** line.

stranger

There is a **stranger** at the door. Nobody knows
who he is. Never open the door to **strangers**.

string

Brambles has saved many pieces of **string**.

stripe

Pa Pig wanted a **striped** suit so
Ali Cat painted **stripes** on it.

strong

Macintosh is **strong**.
He can lift heavy things.

such

Crabbie has **such** big claws no mittens will fit them.

sudden

Haggis was playing his bagpipes. All of a **sudden** they burs

supply   supplies, supplied, supplying

Mamma Bear will not feed the beggars until they have
washed their faces. She **supplied** them with a wash basir
hot water, and a cake of soap.
All they wanted was a big **supply** of food.

suppose supposes, supposed, supposing

Mr. Fixit is **supposed** to mend a leak.
Do you **suppose** he isn't mending it because
he can't get in to find it? Is that the reason?

sure

Mother Cat was **sure** that the little picture hook
wouldn't be strong enough to hold the picture
on the wall. She was certain of it.

surprise surprises, surprised, surprising

Pappa Bear bought a **surprise** present for Mamma.
It was completely unexpected.
It was a cold day so he wore the **surprise** himself.

swallow swallows, swallowed, swallowing

Doctor Pill **swallowed** some medicine
to show Babykins how good it tasted.

sweep sweeps, swept, sweeping

Wiggles is **sweeping** his room.
Sweep it nice and clean, Wiggles!

sweet

Sugar tastes **sweet.**
Lemons taste sour.
Bumbles is putting
a teaspoonful
of lemon on his cereal.

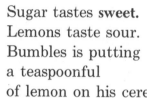
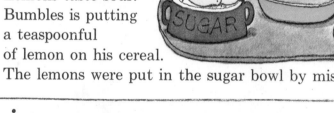

The lemons were put in the sugar bowl by mistake.

swim swims, swam, swum, swimming

Dingo is **swimming** across the river.
He doesn't want his car to get wet.

swing swings, swung, swinging

Crabbie is **swinging** an apple on a string.
Spuds is **swinging** on a **swing.**

terrific!

Tt *Tt*

take takes, took, taken, taking

Haggis is **taking** Heather for a walk.
He **takes** her by the hand.
They are **taking** a picnic with them.

talk talks, talked, talking

Mrs. Fishhead is **talking** to Squeaky.
He is cleaning the inside of her vase.
She is telling him he missed a spot.

tall

Babykins built
a **tall** pile of hats.

taste tastes, tasted, tasting

Andy **tasted** Mamma Bear's soup.
He didn't like the **taste.**
What did you put in the soup, Mamma?

teach teaches, taught, teaching

The **teacher** is **teaching** the children
how to read and write.
Blinky is learning to read.
Macintosh is learning to write.

tear tears, tore, torn, tearing

Wolfson thought he put a piece of pie
in his pocket. He is **tearing** his coat
to pieces trying to find it.

telephone telephones, telephoned, telephoning

Doodledoo **telephoned** Henny on the **telephone**.
He told her to bring out two dozen eggs.
A customer was waiting to buy them.

television

Mr. Fixit is repairing the **television** set.
He is on Channel 2 right now.

tell tells, told, telling

Mother Cat is **telling** Father something.
I wonder if he is listening?

there

Spuds was eating his supper here on the plate.
He is going **there,** across the table,
to get more butter.

they them, their, themselves

What do **they** have? It is **their** present
to Mamma who has been so nice to **them.**
They wrote **their** names all by **themselves.**

thick

Chips is sawing the **thick** branch.

thin

Mr. Fixit is sawing the **thin** branch.
I wonder who will be the first to finish?

thing

What is that **thing** Dingo brought
into the house with him?
The **thing** for him to do is to take it outside.

107

think thinks, thought, thinking thinker

Mose **thought** that an egg would bounce like a rubber ball.
He isn't a very good **thinker.**

this that, these, those

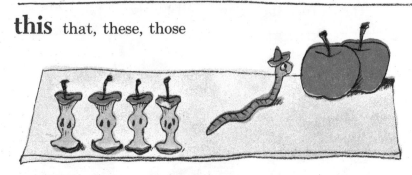

This is a picture of **that** hungry worm, Ooch.
These are the apples he has eaten.
Those farther away are the apples he is about to eat.

though

The piglets are going
to bed even **though** they don't want to.

through

Ali Cat was all **through** with painting
the floor. He was finished.
Then Bumbles walked **through** the room.

throw throws, threw, thrown, throwing

Hooligan **threw** a ball to Ozzie.

Ozzie caught it in his mouth.

ticket

Father Cat has lost his bus **ticket.**

tie ties, tied, tying

Sneakers **tied** his shoelaces.
He **tied** the plimsolls together by mistake.

tight

Pickles' suit is too **tight.** Wiggles' suit is too loose.

time

The clock tells Father what **time** it is.
It is past the **time** he usually leaves
for work. He is late. He doesn't even have
time to change out of his pyjamas.

today

yesterday   **today**   tomorrow

Yesterday the hair tonic bottle was full.
Today it is half full. Tomorrow it will be empty.

together

Mr. Fixit and Chips are working with each other.
Together they hope to fix Dingo's car. Poor Dingo's car!

tool

Mr. Fixit went to the hardware shop
to buy some **tools.** He tried to buy
Crabbie because he thought he was
a new kind of pliers.

hammer

screwdriver

plane

compass

nail   tack   screw

drill

saw

bow saw

monkey wrench

folding ruler

trowel

hoe

pliers

pickaxe

knife

hatchet

jig saw

axe

wheelbarrow

spade

shovel

touch touches, touched, touching

Smiley **touched** the paint to see if it was wet.
It was wet.

tow tows, towed, towing

Whiff's dust lorry had a flat **tyre**.
Mr. Fixit **towed** him to the garage.

toy

GOO GOO
MAMMA   MAMMA

Father gave Babykins a **toy** that walks,
and talks, and even cries
Babykins gave his **toy** a handkerchief
to blow its nose with.

train

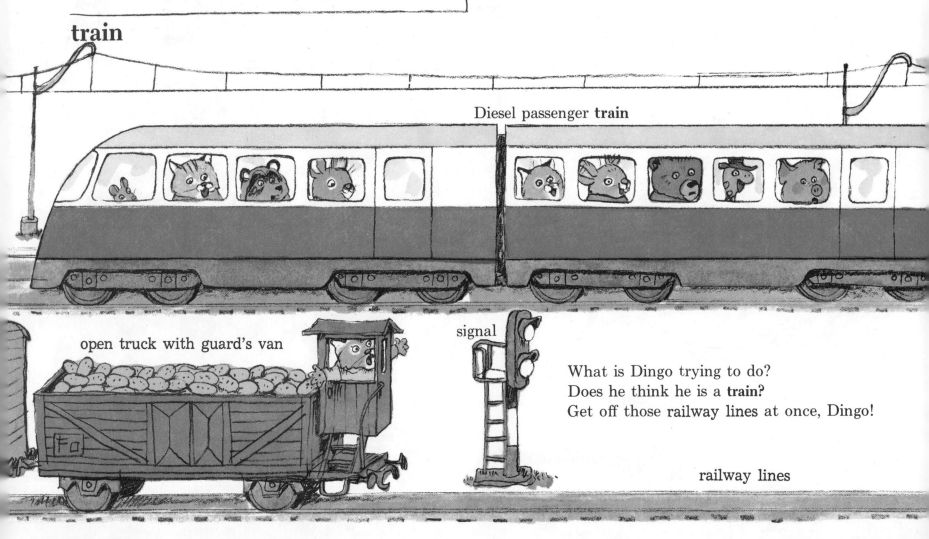

Diesel passenger **train**

open truck with guard's van

signal

What is Dingo trying to do?
Does he think he is a **train?**
Get off those **railway lines** at once, Dingo!

railway lines

goods station

railway station

water tank

station master

platform

yard engine

tanker wagon

coal truck

closed wagon

uffers

Diesel shunter

coach

steam locomotive

electric locomotive

driver

Diesel locomotive

signal box

transport

All these lorries, vans, trailers and buses
are called **transport** because they carry things.
Dingo has a new red racing car.
Look out, all you other drivers,
Look out, you vans and buses.
Oh, that Dingo!

taxi

racing car

police car

breakdown lorry

ambulance

mail van

fire engine

delivery van

estate car

dustman's lorry

jeep

trailer lorry

windscreen
headlight
tail-light
bumper
wheel
steering wheel
tyre

bus

motorcycle

motor scooter

policeman

traffic light

tip lorry

sports car

saloon car

double decker bus

direction sign

tree

twig
branch
leaf
leaves
stem
apple
tree trunk
roots

Macintosh is shaking apples out of the **tree**.
He may shake something else out, too.

trip trips, tripped, tripping

HeeHaw wore a new tie for his **trip** to the city.
It will take him a long time to get there
because he keeps **tripping** over it.

true
truth

It is **true** to say that Mamma bakes cakes.
It is false to say that Mamma bakes cakes
without burning them. She always burns them.
That's the **truth.**

try tries, tried, trying

The beggars were **trying** to find out
if soap was of any good use.
They **tried** eating it and decided
that soap had no good use. **Try** again, boys.

turn turns, turned, turning

Babykins **turned** the watch stem on Father's watch.
He **turned** it too much.
Father **turned** around.

Uu *Uu*

unbelievable!

under

Blinky is learning how to fly.
His engine is running **under** him.

understand understands, understood, understanding

Before Ma Pig went out to get things
for her party, she told Pa Pig to decorate
the house with flowers.
STOP IT, PA! You don't **understand**!
Ma said, FLOWERS—not FLOUR!

until

Grandma knitted a sweater for Kitty.
She knitted **until** she used up all the wool.

up

The sun came **up**.
Doodledoo got **up**.
He buttoned **up** his jacket.
He stood **up** on his toes and said,
"COCK-A-DOODLE-DOO."
Henny wished that he would
shut **up** and let her
sleep until later.

upon

Bully trampled **upon** Ma Pig's flowers.
Macintosh stopped him and put a flower **upon** him.

use uses, used, using

Chips was **using** a sledge hammer
to drive fence posts into the ground.
Oh dear! He missed the fence post.
It is important to **use** tools correctly.

very fine!

Vv

vacation

The Pig family goes to the seaside for summer **vacation** or holiday.

vegetable

HeeHaw grows **vegetables** on his farm.
He is taking them to the market to sell.
My! That is a bumpy road!

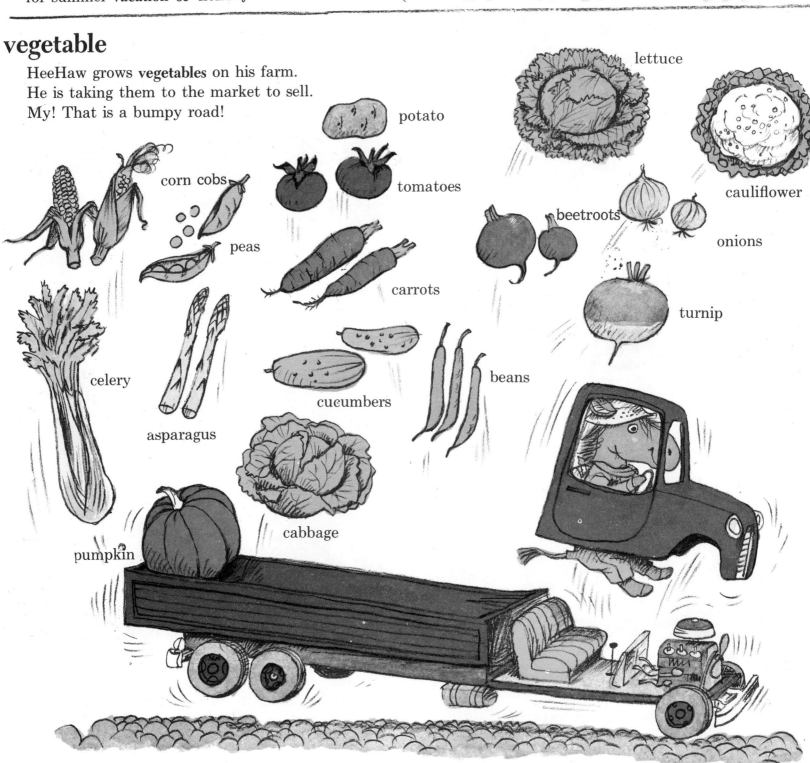

potato

corn cobs

tomatoes

lettuce

cauliflower

peas

beetroots

onions

carrots

turnip

celery

asparagus

cucumbers

beans

pumpkin

cabbage

very

Squeaky sent some box tops away in the post.
Someone sent him a car. It is **very, very** long.

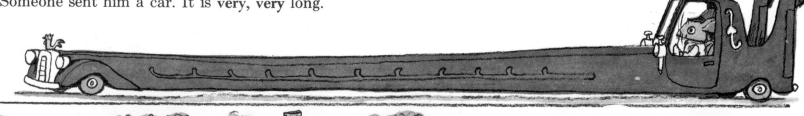

village

Squeaky is driving his car through the little **village**.
Just wait until he gets to the big city.

visit

An old friend of Pappa's came for a **visit**.
He was always laughing out loud.
Pappa's **visitor** stayed for eight weeks.
That's a long **visit**!

voyage

Badger was taking a **voyage** across the sea.
He was taking a long boat trip.
His hat took a **voyage**, too!
As it was leaving, Badger shouted to it
"Write and let me know how you are getting
along on your **voyage**."
He was just being silly, of course.

wow!

Ww Ww

wade wades, waded, wading

Badger went **wading** and didn't get his feet wet.

wait waits, waited, waiting

Dingo is **waiting** for the **red light** to change to GO.

wake wakes, woke, waked, waking

Captain Fishhead was taking a nap.
Bilgy tried to swat a fly.
Captain Fishhead **woke** up.
What a way to **wake.**

walk walks, walking, walked

Wolfson is **walking** to the kitchen with a load of dirty dishes. **Walk** carefully, Wolfson, one foot in front of the other. **Walk,** I said. Don't run. Those are Mama's very best dishes.

want wants, wanted, wanting

BOW WOW!

DOG BISCUITS

Little Chick **wants** Henny to buy him some dog biscuits. They are what he has always **wanted.**

warm

Smiley was cold. He put on some **warm** clothes so that he would be **warm.**

wash washes, washed, washing

Spuds **washes** his food before he eats it.

waste wastes, wasted, wasting

Mummy made many mistakes trying
to make a dress for Flossie.
She **wasted** a lot of material. Such a **waste.**

watch watches, watched, watching

Kitty is baby-sitting.
She is supposed to be **watching** Babykins.
What is she **watching**?

water

Boats sail on **water.**
Rain **water** falls from the sky.
Water comes out of hoses, too.
Water is always wet.

wave waves, waved, waving

Blinky is going on a sea voyage.
He is **waving** good-bye.
The flags are **waving.**
The ocean **waves** are very big.

way

Baron von Crow was lost.
He was a long **way** from home.
He didn't know which **way** to go to get there.
A policeman told him the best **way**
to get home was by taking the train.

we us, our, ourselves, ours

Henny said, "**We** are not all learning
our lesson for today.
One of **us** is reading something else."

119

wear   wears, wore, worn, wearing

The beggars are **wearing** old, **worn**-out trousers.
Somebody **wore** them a long time before
giving them away. Babooby, that isn't the way
to **wear** a pair of trousers!

weather

HeeHaw harvests his grain
in clear, sunny **weather**.

In cloudy, rainy **weather** he gets wet.

In stormy, windy **weather,** when the thunder
rumbles and the lightning flashes,
he hides in the hayloft in the barn.

In wintry **weather,**
when snowflakes fall,
he shovels snow.

In grey, foggy **weather**, he can't see
where he is going, and sometimes
he falls in the well.

weep   weeps, wept, weeping

Mamma is crying loud and long. She is **weeping**
because Pappa Bear told her she couldn't
bake a cake the way his mother could.
Don't **weep**, Mamma. The beggars like your cake.

weigh   weighs, weighed, weighing

Pickles is **weighing** himself.
He can't imagine why he **weighs** so much. Can you?

well

Chips doesn't hit nails very **well**.
Woops! Now his finger doesn't feel very **well**.

what

WHAT HAPPENED????

120

when

When Mamma took the cake out of the oven and saw that it wasn't burned, she fainted. She couldn't believe what she saw.

where

Where has the pie gone?
Point to the spot.

which

Through **which** door did HeeHaw drive out of the barn? **Which** one was it?

while

The barber watched television **while** he cut Brambles' hair. He said that Brambles' hair would grow back in a little **while**.

whisper whispers, whispered, whispering

Blinky **whispered** in Bumbles' ear and told him a secret. Bumbles was not supposed to tell it to anyone, but he **whispered** the secret to Sneakers.
Shame on you, Bumbles. Always keep secrets.

whistle whistles, whistled, whistling

BOW WOW!

Badger is blowing his **whistle**. He can also **whistle** with his lips. Little Chick always comes running when someone **whistles**.

who whom, whose

Who left the boots there?
Whose are they? To **whom** do they belong?

whole

Doodledoo sells eggs.
He has a lot of them, a **whole** basketful.
Careful, Doodledoo. Mamma Bear wants **whole** eggs.
She doesn't want eggs in pieces.

why

Why did Henny cross the street?
Why shouldn't she? She wanted to get to
the other side to find out
why the three beggars were laughing.

will

Squigley tied himself in knots. **Will** he be able
to untie himself, or won't he be able?

win wins, won, winning
winner

Who **won** Mamma Bear's contest
to see who has the dirtiest face?
Wolfson **won** first prize, a cake of soap.
In Mamma's contest everyone is a **winner**.

wind

It is a **windy** day.
Ma Pig's laundry is drying on the line.
The **wind** is blowing very hard.

wind winds, wound, winding

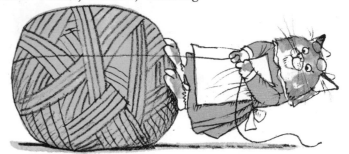

Grandma **winds** her wool into a ball
before she starts to knit a sweater.

wipe wipes, wiped, wiping

Pickles had jam on his face.
He **wiped** it off on his nice, clean shirt.
Oh Pickles! **Wipe** it with a napkin next time.

wish wishes, wished, wishing

Doodledoo **wishes** that he had never
gone for a ride with Baron von Crow.
He would like to be anywhere else.

with
without

Huckle is eating his soup **with** a spoon.
Andy is eating **without** a spoon
He has bad table manners.

wood

woods

axe

stump

saw

log

branch

board

chair

Trees grow in the **woods**.
Trees are made of **wood**.
Chips chopped down the tree.
He is sawing it into boards.

word

BOW WOW!

Little Chick's first **words** were "Bow Wow!"

work works, worked, working

Dingo drove his car into the river on his way to **work**.
Now the car won't **work**.
Mr. Fixit is **working** on it to make it go.
He is a hard **worker**.

123

world

The **world** where we live is round.
And it is filled with a **world**
of wonderful things.

cloud

rain

sky

mountain

hill

valley

river

trees

woods

forest

dandelion seeds

road

police car

fast driver

city

rainbow

fountain

carrot

flower

cobweb

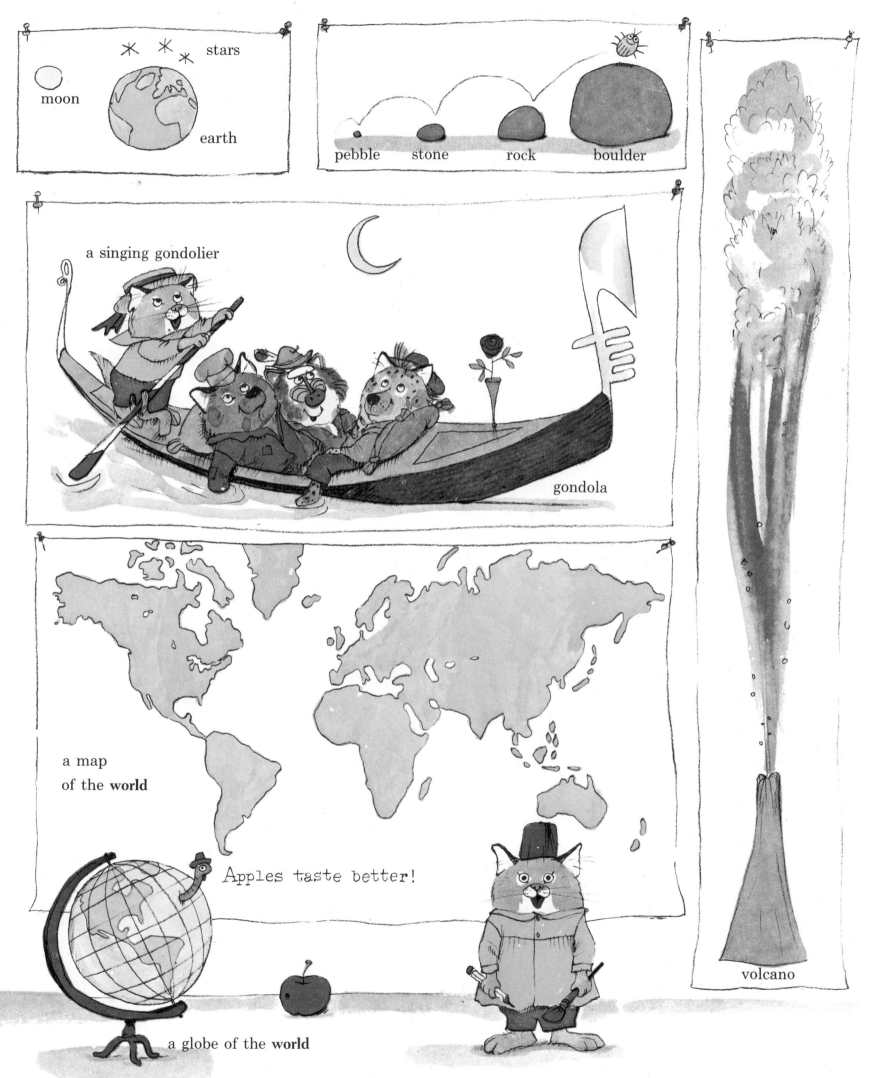

moon

stars

earth

pebble   stone   rock   boulder

a singing gondolier

gondola

a map
of the **world**

Apples taste better!

a globe of the **world**

volcano

125

would

Bilgy **would** like to take Squeaky along for the ride. He **would** if he possibly could. But he can't. There just isn't room.

wreck wrecks, wrecked, wrecking

Dingo **wrecked** his car.
Baron von Crow's plane is a **wreck**, too.

write writes, wrote, written, writing

Fingers is **writing** a letter.
He **wrote** two letters yesterday.

wrong

Chips, you're sawing the board the **wrong** way. Learn the right way or you'll get hurt.

extraordinary!

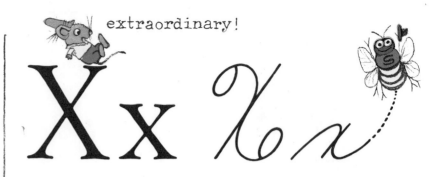

Xx 𝒳𝓍

X-ray

Squigley swallowed something.
Dr. Pill is taking an **X-ray** of Squigley's stomach.

Yy 𝒴𝓎

yippee!

yawn yawns, yawned, yawning

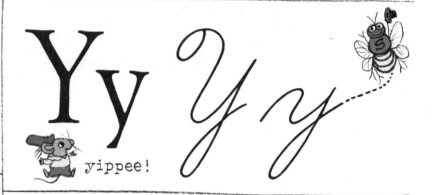

Big Hilda is **yawning**. She is sleepy.

year

Babykins is one **year** old.
How many **years** old are you?

yell yells, yelled, yelling

When Squeaky accidently stepped on Captain Fishhead's tail, the captain **yelled** "OUCH!" What a loud **yell.**

yes

Is HeeHaw planting seeds?
Yes! HeeHaw is planting seeds.

yet

Has Doodledoo broken any eggs today?
No, he hasn't broken any **yet.**

young younger, youngest

Babykins is **young.**
He is **younger** than his brother, Tom.

Zz *Zz*

zoomy!

zigzag

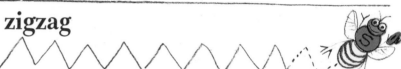

Superbee likes to fly in **zigzags,** up and down.

zip zips, zipped, zipping
zipper

Smiley's **zipper** is stuck.
He is trying to un**zip** it.

zone

Always cross the street in the safety **zone**—
the part marked for walking.

ZZZZZZZ

Superbee goes **zzzzzzz.**

curtains

sun

window

THE NEW DAY

It is the morning of a new day.
The sun is shining.
Little Bear gets up out of bed.

face cloth

soap

towel

First he washes his
face and hands.

toothbrush

toothpaste

Then he brushes
his teeth.

mirror

comb

pyjamas

He combs his hair.

shirt

trousers

He dresses himself.

He makes his bed.

He comes promptly
when he is called to
breakfast.

Bear sits up straight in his chair.

He is very hungry. This is what he eats.

cold fruit juice

warm cereal

with cream

He doesn't eat the toaster.

pancakes

with butter and maple syrup

fried eggs

bacon

toast

muffins

honey

jam

hot cocoa

cool milk

and a waffle

When he finishes eating breakfast he helps his mother to wash and dry the dishes.

cup   saucer   plate   bowl   fork   knife   spoon   glass

jar   jug   frying pan   lid   pot   pan   bottle   juice squeezer   glass

Now he is ready to play with his friends.

THE RABBIT FAMILY'S HOUSE

Father Rabbit, Mother Rabbit, and the
Rabbit Brothers are getting ready for
the new day. Their friend Owl
is waiting for the two brothers
to come out to play.
Can you find him?

chimney

roof

mirror

father

lamp

bed

bedroom

cupboard

dining
room

table

kitchen

sink

back door

chair

floo

axe

stove

mother

woodpile

lawn

bird bath

WHOO

owl

smoke

television
aerial

light
switch

television set

record player

bunk bed

bathroom

landing

boys' bedroom

front door

living room

candle

outside
light

picture

telephone

fireplace

stairs

sofa

front
hall

door mat

rug

window

stone path

AT THE PLAYGROUND

The children are all having fun doing different things. Which children are doing the things you like best?

see-saw

slide

leapfrog

somersault

hide-and-seek

ring-a-ring-o'-roses

skipping rope

ladder

rings

swing

sliding pole

top

roller skates

bubble blowing

kite

jungle gym

merry-go-round

tag

tossing the ring

hoop rolling

jacks

marbles

sand pit

kite string

bouncing ball

hopscotch

133

hammer

nail

TOOLS

Everyone is very busy
working with his tools.
Who always carries his
tool with him?
He has a red head.

chart pin

axe

carpenter

board

sandpaper

ladder

log

sawdust

hacksaw

drill

plane

woodpecker

jig saw

wood shavings

screwdriver

screws

file

pliers

bowsaw

trowel

bricklayer

hoe

brick

brick wall

cement

timber

fence painter

paint brush

ball of twine

saw horse

barrel

paint

tack

tack hammer

hatchet

ruler

folding ruler

jackknife

tool box

square

putty knife

shovel

bolt

nut

earth

monkey wrench

compass

wheelbarrow

pick axe

glue

haystack

cow

apple tree

farmhouse

water pump

meadow

fence

sheep

horse

clothes-line

apple

grass

clothes basket

FARMER BEAR'S FARM

Farmer Bear has a very busy farm.

What is Mrs Bear doing? What is the horse doing?

What is the duck doing?

What is the scarecrow
supposed to be doing? He is
not doing it, is he?

FRESH
HONEY
AND
EGGS

chicken house

well

duck pond

bee

duck   ducklings

pitchfork

beehive

weather instruments

blimp

control tower

microphone

helicopter

AT THE AIRPORT

The man in the control tower is talking
into his microphone. He is talking to the
handsome pilot by radio. He is telling him
that he will have nice weather on his flight.

baggage train

waiting
room

binoculars

tourist

camera

observation deck

jet plane

wind sock

runway

hangar

runway lights

light plane

propeller

mechanic

jet military plane

jet passenger plane

handsome pilot

baggage man

tail

pretty stewardess

fuselage

wing

baggage loader

jet engine

passenger-loading stairs

139

TOYS

When you play with toys, it is more fun
if you share them with your friends.
When you play games you may win and
sometimes you may lose. Bear is a good sport.
He is losing a game but he might
win the next time.
Do you think he might
win the next game?

tricycle

teddy bear

electric trains

doll

blocks

lorry and loader

Bear is losing.

game

Rabbit is winning.

building set

140

castle

croquet

toy soldiers

tea set

racing car

robot

typewriter

bean bags

doll's house

rocking horse

scooter

glider

bow and arrow

hook

ham

saw

scales

MEATS

wrapping paper

twine

meat cleaver

butcher

pickle barrel

bologna

frankfurters

hamburger

fish

bacon

chop

dustbin

steak

a piglet who wants to be a butcher when he grows up

cart

sawdust

AT THE SUPERMARKET

Mrs Pig is buying groceries for her family.
What would you like to buy the next time
you go to the market?
Would you like to buy a pickle?

books

customer

orange juice

raisins

money

handbag

eggs

milk

cashier

yoghourt

butter

142

cash register

FRUITS

pineapple

apples

oranges

pears

grapefruit

melons

grapes

lemons

cherries

strawberries

raspberries

bilberries

plums

bananas

scales

grocer

VEGETABLES

corn

beans

lettuce

tomatoes

peas

spinach

potatoes

asparagus

celery

onions

cabbage

beets

peaches

cauliflower

carrots

cucumbers

watermelon

coconut

turnip

broom

biscuits

sugar

cereal

spaghetti

tinned food

peanut butter

cheese

salt

apricots

baby food

bread

jam

143

MEALTIME

Father Pig, Mother Pig, and
Peter Pig love to eat. There
is so much food on the table
it is hard to find Peter.
Can you find him?

carving knife and fork

roast beef

meat dish

coffee pot

tablespoon

teapot

salt cellar

pepper pot

fork

dinner plate

glass

cream jug

cup

knife

saucer

spoon

napkin

sugar bowl

turkey

milk jug

cake

green beans

blancmange

baked potatoes

cranberry jelly

mashed swede

mashed potatoes

onions

beetroots

ice cream

peas

butter

steak

soup

pie

salad

white bread

rye bread

rolls

145

smokestack

submarine

stern

ocean liner

bow

tug

police boat

barge

ferry boat

pirate ship

BOATS AND SHIPS

What do you see in the water which is not
a boat? It helps boats find
the place they want to go.

motor boat

paddle

canoe

kayak

oar   rowing boat

freighter

lightship

AMBROSE

CG-7

launch

oil tanker

fireboat

fishing nets

sport fishing-boat

fishing trawler

speedboat

houseboat

raft

GRETEL

yacht

lightbuoy

2

147

KEEPING HEALTHY

Your doctor and your dentist are two of your very best friends. They want to help you to stay strong, healthy, and happy. Will you give your doctor and dentist a great big smile the next time you see them? How big can you smile?

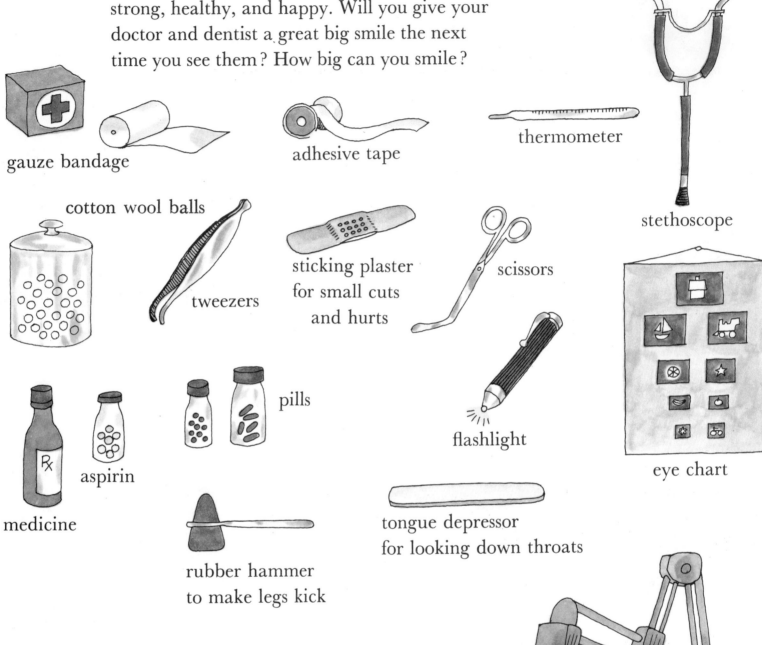

gauze bandage

adhesive tape

thermometer

stethoscope

cotton wool balls

tweezers

sticking plaster for small cuts and hurts

scissors

flashlight

eye chart

pills

medicine

aspirin

rubber hammer to make legs kick

tongue depressor for looking down throats

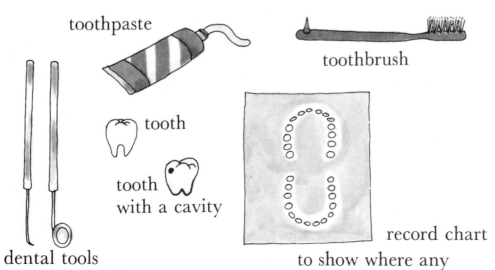

toothpaste

toothbrush

dental tools

tooth

tooth with a cavity

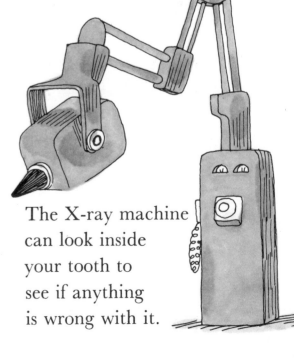

record chart to show where any cavities have been found

The X-ray machine can look inside your tooth to see if anything is wrong with it.

At the doctor's surgery

nurse

test tube

scales

hurt tail

patient

doctor

dental drill

dentist

mouth-rinse bowl

instrument table

water cup

At the dentist's surgery

dentist's chair

dental unit

dental nurse

The dental nurse hasn't a cavity in her teeth.
Brush your teeth well and you may not get any.

149

THE BEAR TWINS GET DRESSED

Brother Bear woke up one cold, frosty morning.
He wanted to dress very warmly before
he went outside.

He yawned and got up out of bed.

He took off his pyjamas
and left them on the floor.
Naughty bear!

pyjama
top

pyjama
bottom

slippers

He put on his

  cap

underwear

shirt

trousers

overalls

socks

hat

plimsolls

gloves

tie

sweater

muffler

jacket

overcoat

raincoat

and sou'wester

As he was walking out of the front door
his Mother said, 'Don't forget
to put your boots on!'

boots

Sister Bear got up out of bed.

She took off her pretty nightgown and put it away neatly. Nice bear!

nightgown

She put on her   panties

petticoat

hair ribbon

            ear muffs

blouse   skirt   pinafore   stockings   shoes

snow suit   and mittens.

She put her handkerchief

and purse   in her handbag

As she was walking out of the front door her mother said, 'Don't forget to put your boots on!'

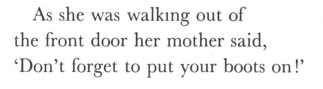

Do you ever forget to put on your boots?

deer

lion

elephant

tiger

panda

monkeys

brown bear

gorilla

polar bear

152

buffalo

camel

zebra

zoo keeper

giraffe

leopard

sealion

rhinoceros

zoo train

AT THE ZOO

Mr and Mrs Mouse took
their children to the zoo.
How will those children
ever be able to get
all those balloons
into their house tonight?
Which is your favourite animal
at the zoo?

hippopotamus

NUMBERS

How high can you count?
Can you count up to
twenty ladybirds?
I'll bet you can.

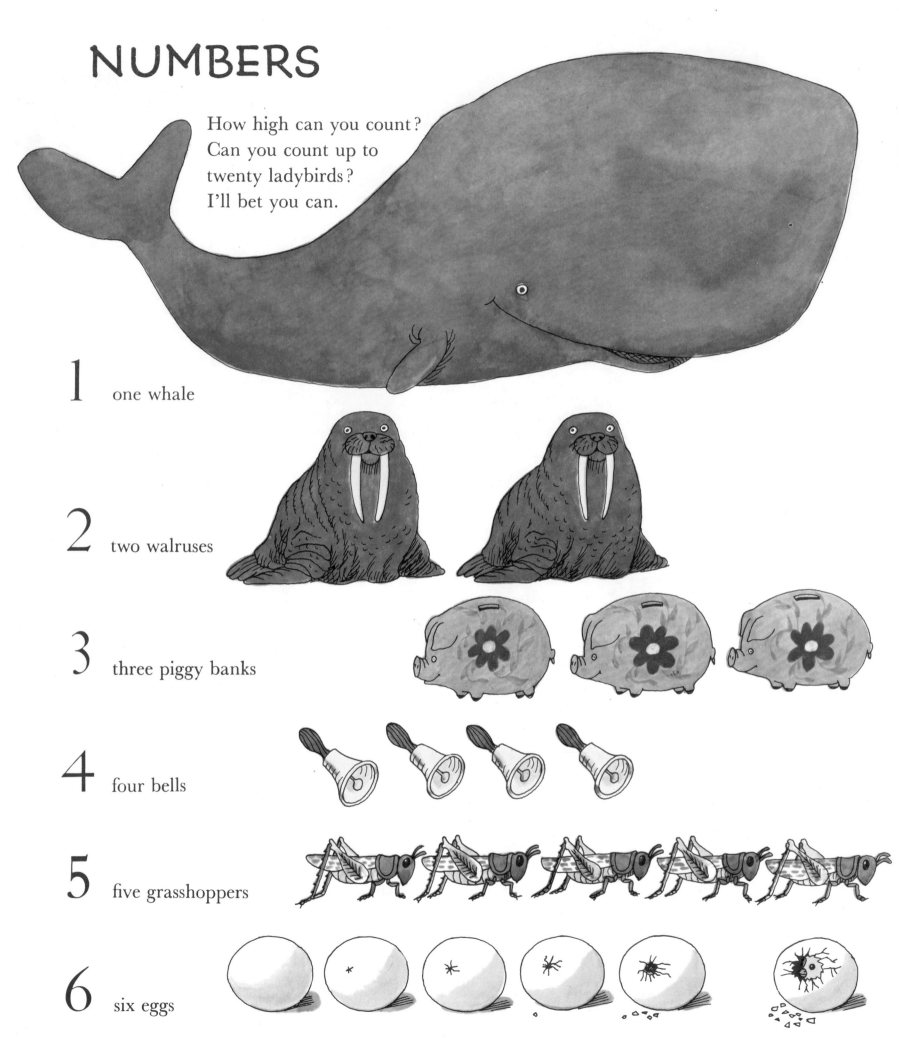

1 one whale

2 two walruses

3 three piggy banks

4 four bells

5 five grasshoppers

6 six eggs

7   seven caterpillars

8   eight reels

9   nine spiders

10   ten keys

11   eleven ants

12   twelve rings

13   thirteen sweets

14   fourteen leaves

15   fifteen snowflakes

16   sixteen acorns

17   seventeen pins

18   eighteen buttons

19   nineteen beads

20   twenty ladybirds

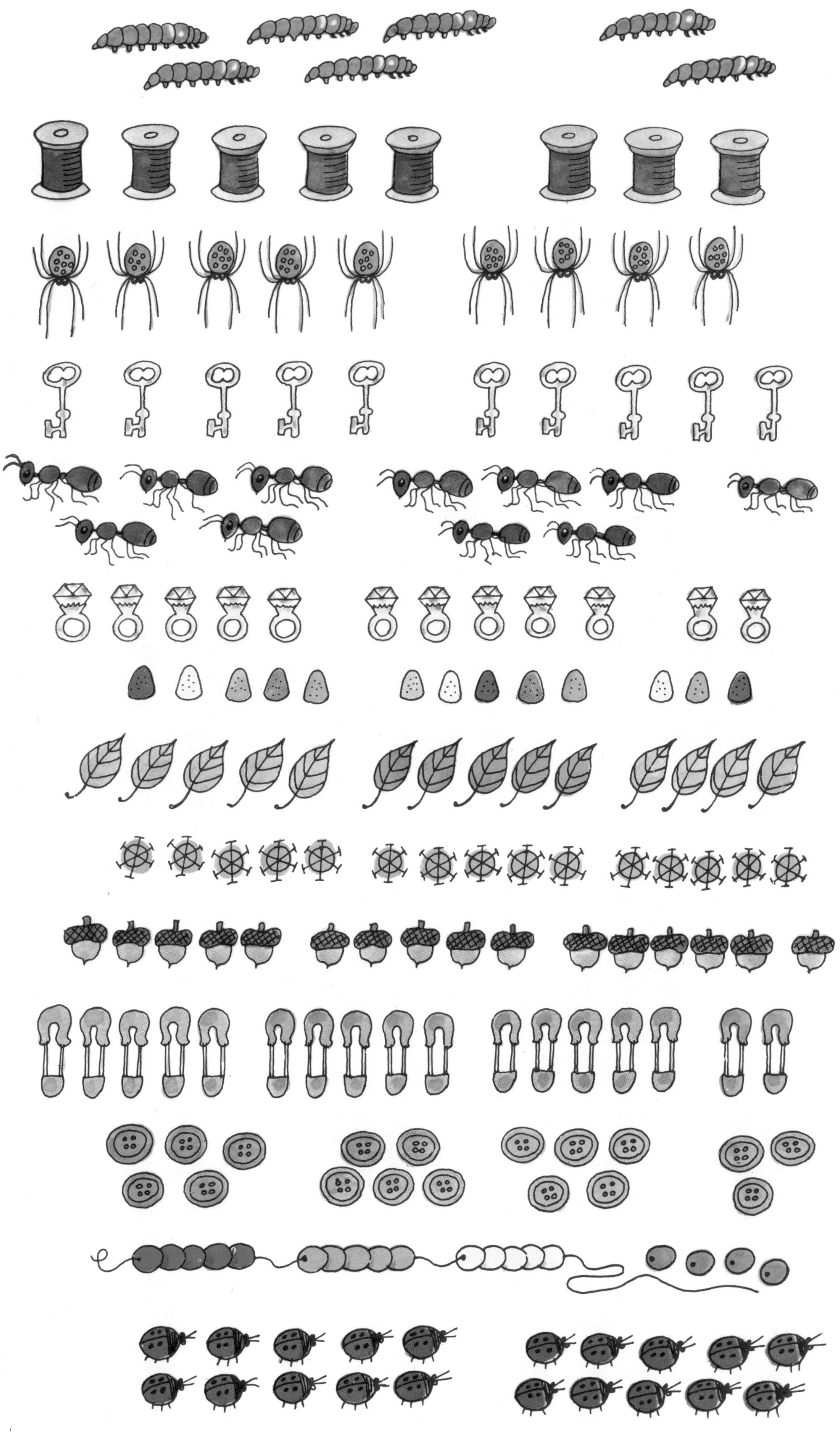

MUSIC MAKING

The conductor leads the orchestra by waving his baton. The musicians are playing a very gay tune.
Which of the musical instruments do you think you could learn to play?

double bass

bassoon

cello

oboe

clarinet

flute

piccolo

violin

baton

conductor

viola

piano

notes

podium

kettle drums

snare drum

bass drum

cymbals

triangle

saxophone

French horn

trumpet

tuba

tambourine

cornet

trombone

banjo

guitar

harp

accordion

harmonica

comb and tissue paper

157

BOOK PUBLISHER

editor

COSTUMES

skyscraper

aerial

church

NEWSPAPER OFFICE

Dancing School

traffic lights

flats

telephone box

Book Shop

CHEMIST

book reader

van

street

IN THE CITY

Mouse has just bought a book at the book shop. He is going to buy a newspaper and then join his rabbit friends at the café and drink some lemonade with them. Show with your finger the way he will go. Remember to make him look both ways before he crosses a street.

158

hotel

street sign

park

park
bench

statue

taxi

RESTAURANT

manhole

DANGER

one
way

barber's
shop

café

delivery man

police car

THEATRE

NOW PLAYING

Mis

CA

TAXI

bus

pavement

underground entrance

newspapers

newsagent

underground
station

A DRIVE
IN THE COUNTRY

There are many things to see when
you take a drive in the country.
Can you see what the mountain climber
has dropped out of his knapsack?

radio tower

ocean

island

factory

petrol station

lake

tunnel

petrol pump

toll gate

motorway

bridge

brook

farm

mill

waterfall

stream

layby

picnickers

lighthouse

beach

bay

woods

harbour

crane

fire lookout tower

drawbridge

hill

windmill

village

tug

mountain

river

pond

log cabin

road

forest

mountain climber

knapsack

cliff

apple

AT SCHOOL

School is fun. There are so many things we learn to do. Little Bear is learning how to find a lost glove.

pencil sharpener

chalk

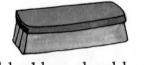
blackboard rubber

notebook

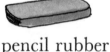
pencil rubber

pencil

pen

ball-point pen

paper

straw

milk

ink

biscuits

scissors

string

yarn

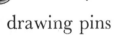
paper clip

paste

exercise book

storybook

drawing pins

modelling clay

lost-clothing drawer

 clock

 bell

blackboard

calendar

teacher

map

map stand

inkwell

waste-paper basket

artist

pupil

desk

classroom

paper dolls

headmaster

refrigerator

kitchen cabinet

door knob

tin opener

soap

teapot

light socket

work surface

freezer

refuse bin

clothes-washer

dish-washer

laundry basket

egg beater

stool

egg shells

spoon

measuring jug

mixing bowl

rolling pin

strainer

biscuit cutter

dough

cake tin

funnel

baking tray

sauce bottle

slice

flour bin

sugar bowl

mustard pot

mincer

164

broom cupboard

feather duster

broom

mop

dust pan

vacuum cleaner

egg timer

shelf

fly swatter

hood

coffee pot

burner

kettle

stove

oven

iron

ironing board

IN THE KITCHEN

All the little piglets like to help their mother in the kitchen. They are making good things to eat. What is Mother Pig putting into the oven?

teaspoon

tablespoon

soupspoon

double boiler

blender

pestle

toaster

corkscrew

ladle

mortar

saucepan

colander

cutting board

electric mixer

potato masher

measuring spoons

salt cellar

matches

pepper mill

cookery book

carving fork and knife

THINGS WE DO

There are many things
that we can do. And there
are some things we cannot do.
What is one thing we can't do?
Look and see.

dig

blow

build

break

sleep

wake up

walk

run

stand

sit

read

watch

draw and write

166

pull

push

kick

talk

listen

shout

whisper

eat

laugh

smile

cry

drink

jump over

crawl under

fall down

we can't fly

raise a hat

peep

go up

go down

go in

come out

167

car transporter

petrol tanker

electric van

saloon car

breakdown lorry

motorcycle

taxi

sports car

TAXI

WORLD-WIDE REMOVALS

trailer van

CARS AND LORRIES

Down the street go the
cars and lorries.
But look! Some of the
cars don't have drivers.
Which cars have no drivers?

dustcart

boat trailer

station wagon

motor scooter

SCHOOL BUS

vintage car

school bus

HOTEL

GENERAL STORE
COWBOY SUITS

BOOTS

BANK

TOWN HALL

street lamp

hitching post

gold miner

burro

cowboy

sheriff

money box

frontier locomotive

headlight

BUFFALO BILL

stagecoach

wheel

cowcatcher

OUT WEST

Indian is coming to town to buy
a horse for his squaw to ride.
Why do you think it
would be nice for her to
have a horse to ride?

covered wagon

dust

saddle

oxen

BLACKSMITH

horseshoe

Indian

papoose

squaw

HAY
FEED
AND GRAIN

barrel

lasso

cattle truck

tender

cattle

corral

cowpony

round

square

triangle

diamond

star

crescent

heart

straight

curved

SHAPES AND SIZES

cone

big

little

fat

tiny

thin

short

tall

short

long

172

THE BABY

father

mother

grandmother

uncle

That cat family has a new baby kitten.
They don't know what to name it.
What would you like
to name the new baby?
Write the kitten's name here.

_ _ _ _ _ _ _ _ _

grandfather

rattle

sister

baby

nappy

playpen

bottle

brother

aunt

high chair

cot

cousin

pushchair

cradle

play table

walker

pram

173

AT THE CIRCUS

The band is playing and the animals are doing their acts. What do you like to watch best at the circus?

tent pole

balancing pole

tightrope performer

tightrope

bareback rider

band

rope ladder

bandstand

circus horse

performing elephant

sawdust

ring

ringmaster

performing dog

clown

pennant

circus tent

trapeze

trapeze artist

acrobat

safety net

ticket seller

hoop

lion

whip

lion tamer

cage

juggler

trained sealion

balloon man

popcorn man

175

TRAINS

Which train do you think
would be the most fun to run?
Would it be a goods train
or a passenger train?

signal

lantern

hand trolley

guard's van

flatbed

dining car

railway station

platform

luggage trolley

guard

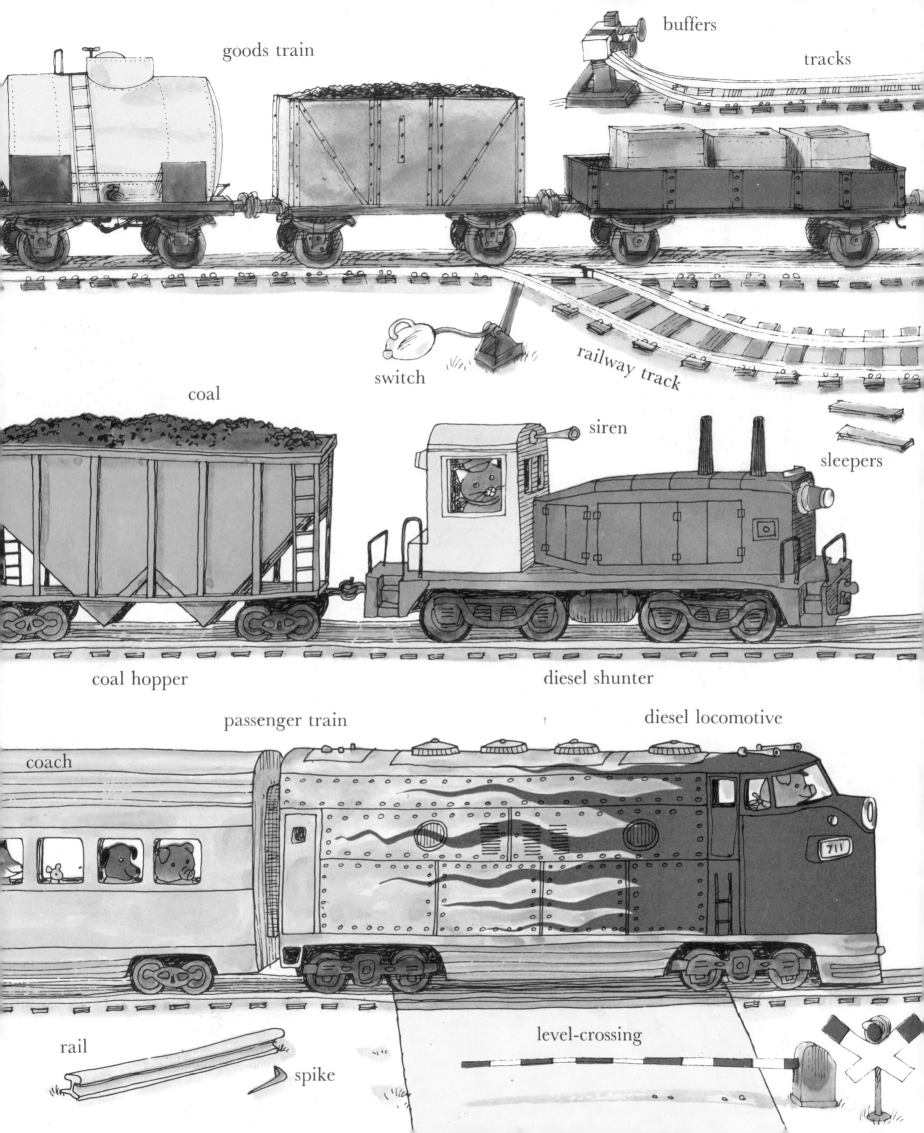

goods train

buffers

tracks

switch

railway track

coal

siren

sleepers

coal hopper

diesel shunter

passenger train

diesel locomotive

coach

711

rail

spike

level-crossing

AT THE BEACH

In the summertime it is fun
to go to the beach.
What do you think
Rabbit hears in the seashell?
Is it the sound of the waves?

telescope

lighthouse

summer cottage

anchor

beach toy

oar

spade

rowing boat

sandpiper

sand castle

skate

mackerel

oyster

lobster

sea purse

scallop

hermit crab

clam

CLEANING-UP TIME

Each of the animals has a job to do to make everything tidy around the house. What do you think each animal is about to do?

mop

cleaning powder

glue

sponge

spilled water

coat hanger

wrench

waste paper

bag of nails

eyeglasses

octopus who sews

hammer

torn bed-sheet

sewing machine

muddy boots

footprints

chipped vase

chip

paw prints on the wall

clothes rail

wire coat hangers

broken table leg

leaking tap

brush

dust pan

wastepaper-basket

fireplace ashes

book

bookcase

old newspapers

old magazines

wire coat hangers

dustbin

Don't you think some of them should be thrown in the dustbin?

kite

rain shower

plough

bird

nest

buds

SPRING

Look at that baby lamb hop!
It is spring. He is happy.
Look at Mr Bear coming out of
his cave! It is spring.
Now he can use his new
lawn mower.

tree

lamb

bush

bridge

brook

cave

fern

tortoise

roots

pussy willow

daffodil

lawn mower

violets

crocus

cow

meadow

cornfield

calf

fence

SUMMER

Do you like to go
on picnics in the summer time?
Ants just love to go to picnics.
Do you know why?

station wagon

tent

fly

camp bed

cooking grill

screen

charcoal

water carrier

picnic basket

hamburger

charcoal bag

hotdog

mosquito

fishing rod

gherkin

mustard   ketchup

paper cup

rock

ants

float

landing stage

bulrushes

pond

frog

water lily

dragonfly

pebbles

stones

183

sun

falling leaves

pheasant

gate

stone wall

grou

nuts

roadside stand

maize cobs

cider

jam

AUTUMN

In the autumn the air gets
colder. The green leaves turn to
bright colours. Then they fall to
the ground. Who is raking
them all up?

smoke

flames

turkey

basket of app

rake

bonfire

184   leaves

snowstorm

WINTER

There are many ways to
have fun on the snow and ice.
Maybe you would like to do
all of them. Would you?

sleigh

icicle

fishing
hut

ice fishing

skis

sledge

toboggan

ice-skating rink

snowball

hockey stick

puck

ice skates

uffler

are tyre

jeep

snowplough

a pig all wrapped up

pipe

snowman

BEDTIME

Who is that hiding under the bed?
Find the naughty rascal and tell him to brush his
teeth and get into bed.

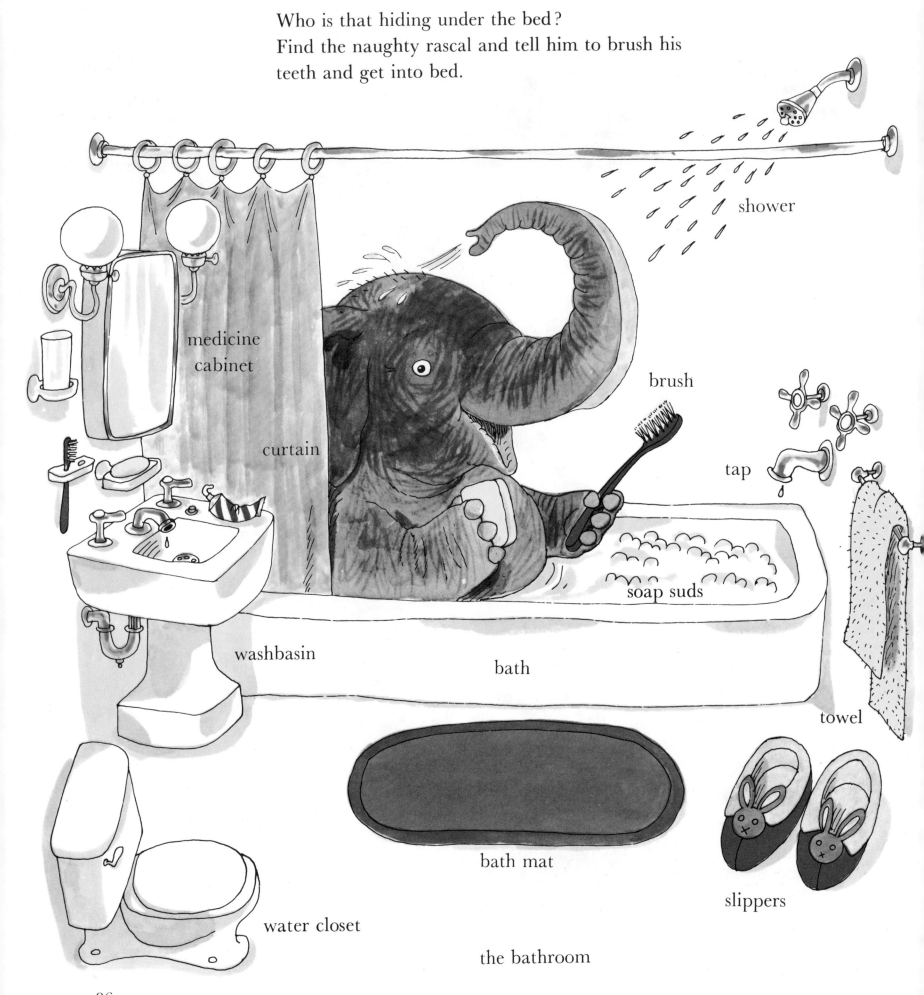

shower

medicine
cabinet

brush

curtain

tap

soap suds

washbasin

bath

towel

bath mat

slippers

water closet

the bathroom

THE LAST WORDS OF THE DAY

The animals have a last word to say
before they go to bed.

cheep

oink

bow-wow

meow

cut-cut

gruff

sniff-sniff

yipe

quack

squeek

whoo

chug-a-room

Do you know what they are saying?
They are saying 'Good night'.

galumpf, galumpf, galumpf

Walrus has some last words, too.
Do you know what he is saying?

sun

falling leaves

pheasan

gate

stone wall

gro

nuts

roadside stand

maize cob

cider

jam

smoke

flames

turkey

basket of app

rake

bonfire

leaves